MW01256829

"The book is wildly valuable. It should be required reading for anyone leading or desiring to lead. It expertly breaks down the leadership journey into components that can be studied, understood, and thus mastered. We all know that trying to be a better leader is ineffective; this book helps the reader understand the individual elements that make up the full equation."

—**Dan Simons**, Founder & CEO,
Founding Farmers, Inc.

"This book is fantastic. It's the practical guide, a path . . . or more appropriate, the formula that I am using to improve and try to become better, the best leader I can be."

—**Steve Newton**,
Founder & CEO, Mission BBQ, Inc.

"This book forced me to check in on my own leadership attributes and the culture I'm building in our company. I thank DeCotiis for providing an actionable piece of literature and the five questions every leader needs to address. This will help me re-focus on leadership, personal character, and values within my business."

—**Jeremy L. Davis**, Managing Director,
Ameriprise Financial Services, Inc.

"The book makes being an adored leader tangible, actionable, and achievable for all through the establishment of the right habits. DeCotiis is a fantastic storyteller and that differentiates [him] from many others who write about leadership. Multiple industry examples help people see that these principles resonate regardless of the company, role, or expertise."

—**Jennifer Saavedra**, PhD, SVP, Human Resources,
Global Sales, Dell, Inc.

"Tom's book inspired me to think long and hard about the sense of belonging and significance we create for the most valuable asset we have: our people. Anyone looking to step up their leadership game should absolutely take advantage of this insightful look into taking [their] skills to the next level. Its groundbreaking insights are a refreshing and inspiring reminder that leadership character is truly the root of all results."

—**Casey Hinson**, Director, Training & Development,
Metro Diner, Inc.

"I read [the book] straight through and found it insightful. I appreciate the care and thoughtfulness that DeCotiis puts into the words he chooses, the use of the models, the brisk pacing, [and] the more casual and personal point of view. Teaching in a familiar tone and using personal stories resonates."

—**Wyman Roberts**, Chairman and CEO,
Brinker International, Inc.

"Tom DeCotiis is among the very few whose intellect easily streams into fluent, actionable ideas. Beyond assumptive factors such as simple respect, in *Adored* Tom reveals the formula sculpting the inspiring, follow-anywhere leader, with real-world examples of how the sum of this equation directly telegraphs above-market success for teams, team members, and enterprises."

—**Steve Cranford**, Creative Chairman & CEO,
WHISPER globally, New York

ADORED

THE LEADER
YOUR TEAM
NEEDS YOU
TO BE

ADORED

THE LEADER YOUR TEAM NEEDS YOU TO BE

TOM DeCOTIIS, PHD

CharacterPress
Colorado Springs, CO

Published by CharacterPress
Colorado Springs, CO

Distributed by Greenleaf Book Group

For ordering information or special discounts for bulk purchases, please contact
Greenleaf Book Group at PO Box 91869, Austin, TX 78709, 512.891.6100.

Design and composition by Greenleaf Book Group and Kimberly Lance
Cover design by WHISPER

Publisher's Cataloging-in-Publication data is available.

Print ISBN: 978-0-578-73740-9

eBook ISBN: 978-0-578-73741-6

Part of the Tree Neutral® program, which offsets the number of trees consumed in the
production and printing of this book by taking proactive steps, such as planting trees
in direct proportion to the number of trees used: www.treeneutral.com

TreeNeutral

Printed in the United States of America on acid-free paper

20 21 22 23 24 25   10 9 8 7 6 5 4 3 2 1

First Edition

Dedicated to the Adored Leaders I have known.

THE LESS EGO YOU BRING TO THE TABLE,
THE BETTER YOUR TEAM EATS.

a•dore [uh-dawr, uh-dohr] *v.* to regard with the utmost esteem, love, and respect; to honor.

CONTENTS

AUTHOR'S NOTE

I use a term in the following pages to describe an exceptionally good leader. The word is "adored." There: I've said it, and you have been forewarned. I warn you because more than a few of the people who read early drafts of this book said they were uncomfortable with the word. Most of them were helpful, suggesting alternatives such as "great" or "revered." They warned me away from calling them Adored Leaders, implying that the term was not only too unique an application, but it was also just plain weird. They have a point, as this is likely the first book you have read to use "adored" as a way to describe a leader.

One reviewer was miffed by the use of the word, saying that "adored" was wrong because "that's what President Trump wants to be." I waved that one off for reasons of common sense: President Trump is no different than almost every other politician—today or ever. It seems to me that all politicians are in the "adore-me" business. That's not a knock on politicians, as a psychologist will tell you that most people are in the adore-me business to some extent. In fact, saying that people crave adoration is not too strong a claim.

It's natural to crave something that makes us feel good. It's just that as we grow from a pin-my-pictures-on-the-fridge tyke to a self-contained adult, we learn to be a bit more subtle about our need for adoration—but the need never goes away. However, I digress, as my choice of the term goes a bit deeper than politics or human need to the heart of what the best leaders always do: *make a positive difference in the lives of others.*

I avoided using the word "great" in my first book, and I'm committed to doing the same in this one. It's a descriptor that is way overused and, frankly, adds no more clarity to the conversation about leadership than do many other frequently used business terms, like "the brand" or "exceed expectations." Take "exceed expectations" as an example: you're having lunch, and the restaurant manager drops by your table and asks, "How is everything?" You reply, "Great!" Was it really great, or are you just being polite, or do you want to be left alone? Was it among your top three lunch experiences of all time, or was it simply good? Was it a match with the restaurant's social media ratings or better or worse? Did it reach that threshold of exceeding expectations, or were you just fueling up, having no expectations except not to be hungry when you finished?

There are a few factors that affect how you answer mindless questions like these. The first one is your standards. If your standards are low, and therefore easily exceeded, it might be a great lunch, even when your friend is complaining about the same meal. Another factor is your mood. If you're just in a terrific mood and everything seems to be going your way, so will the meal. Still another is your experience. If you're like me and have worked with restaurateurs for more than fifty years, you know quality ingredients and skilled preparation when you see it. What is truly descriptive of your experience? Who knows? What I do know is that words like "great" are sloppy words that very often leave too much wiggle room with respect to the value of something. It's like asking, "How high is high?" If you are five feet tall, high is likely to be a lot lower than if you are seven feet tall.

INTRODUCTION

GREAT OR SORT OF GREAT?

George Washington is generally recognized as the father of our country, and it is a consensus among historians that he was a *great* president. Well, there is also the fact that he owned more than two hundred slaves and learned his generalship through trial and error (at the cost of many American lives). Sure, you say, but he saved the country when (arguably) no one else could have done the job. Besides that, he insisted that the office of president of the United States be limited to two terms, perhaps saving us from a lifetime ruler. You might laugh at that conclusion, but some of his contemporaries wanted him to take the title "Emperor" and be called "His Excellency." Besides that, he freed his slaves upon his death. So maybe we can agree that he was "sort of" great.

Some say that Barack Obama was a *great* president. Others would reply, "Yeah, but . . ." to that statement, taking exception to his drawing provocative but unenforced red lines in Syria, managing the slowest economic recovery in US history, and governing largely by executive order. But he was the first African-American president, you say, very intelligent, and single-handedly solved the health-care crisis—except that it's still a crisis. So let's say that he was "sort of" great too.

President Donald J. Trump was impeached by the House of Representatives in December 2019, found not guilty by the Senate on February 5, 2020, and hit an all-time high (49 percent) popularity rating the next day. Something for everyone to love or to hate. So it is that some Americans think he's done a *great* job, while some other Americans think he's deplorable and should be drummed out of office, and still others have never accepted his election in the first place and feel so strongly about it that they have vowed to resist his presidency through whatever means possible. Yeah, you might say, but he has mostly kept his campaign promises better than any other contemporary president, has substantially reduced regulation, gets things done, raised the standard of living for most Americans, and is the first "Tweeter-in-Chief." He also can be obnoxious, play it loose with the truth, and is totally self-centered. So let's say that he is "sort of" great too.

These are three leaders doing the same job with several different interpretations of their contributions. Who's right? Who's wrong? Who knows? Who cares? But it does matter. My point: "great" is a description that depends way too much upon your perspective and context, unless it's applied to something so incredibly unique and superbly executed that its greatness is inarguable.

Leonardo's *Mona Lisa* meets that standard, but I did not say "great" the first time I saw it. I distinctly remember saying to myself, "Perfect; absolutely perfect." I said the same thing the first time I saw Michelangelo's *David* in Florence, Italy. I was humbled and awed by its beauty and the skill of its creator; it's as though the statue was in the stone and Michelangelo simply released it. I was doubly impressed after I learned that he carved *David* from a piece of marble of such poor quality that every other sculptor in Florence had rejected it as unworkable. *David* did not exceed my expectations, as I had no idea what to expect before I saw it in person, but it did blow me away. The same goes for Leonardo's *Mona Lisa*. Both will leave you awed, but I'm pretty sure that you will not describe them as great. It is too weak and shallow a word in the presence of true awesomeness—or, dare I say, perfection or something to be adored.

ADORED IS MORE THAN A WORD—IT'S AN EXPERIENCE

I have worked with a lot of leaders over the course of my long career. A handful of them were incompetent—some breathtakingly so. These leaders did more harm than good and never grew beyond being what I call an "appointed leader": they had the job, but it was always a breath of fresh air to their team when one of these misfits was replaced. More typically, I have worked with "accepted leaders." These leaders had the best of intentions, cared about the organization and their team, worked hard, and usually got the job done. While they made a difference, they were not *the* difference-maker in terms of their team's success. They were more like cogs in a leadership wheel, one more successor in a chain of succession.

Then there were those few who made me wonder, "How did they do that?" and who were described by those around them as "talented" or "bringing something special to the table." They blew me away with their energy, insight, and ability to get people to enthusiastically and consistently be their best. They were memorable for the right reasons, trusted from all angles, and inevitably lifted the spirits of their team. I call them "Adored Leaders." I like precise words, and this is a perfect fit with the dictionary definition of "adore" on the title page of this book: "to regard with the utmost esteem, love, and respect; to honor." (Before I go further, I have to clarify the use of the term "love," as a few of my friends said that using the term in the context of leadership made them uncomfortable. Love, in the context of an Adored Leader, means "acting for the well-being and satisfaction of others." It's what all of us do when we care about someone.) I have worked with a lot of leaders who could have been adored, but weren't. That's because their egos got in the way. Some had to have all the credit, others lost sight of what made them successful, and still others simply got rich and lost interest in the hard work of leadership. Your ego wants to be adored, but that is the opposite of being an Adored Leader. That's because in order to be adored by your team, you have to let go of your ego. For when your ego falls away, as a leader you flourish along with your team.

None of the Adored Leaders I have known were easy to work with. They were demanding, but at the same time they were caring and held in the utmost esteem by their team. This does not mean that they were always likeable: most of them had a temper that they (largely) managed, were fond of their own ideas, and were extremely competitive. These leaders changed their teams in significant ways and made it much better for everyone. When they left, they always left a hole in the team that could not easily be filled.

I have a dear friend who shares my love of words. While he's not exactly obsessed with using the correct word in the right place, he's pretty close. Okay, he's obsessed. Dick and I have been friends for more than forty years and love our little debates over which word is best—particularly with a glass or two of fine wine to warm the discussion. So when I started writing this book, I naturally sent the introduction to Dick, only to receive an email in return forcefully suggesting that I change "adored" to "revered." He immediately pulled out the big gun, citing none other than the late Samuel I. Hayakawa—a world-renowned semanticist and a mutual hero of ours. Despite the flak I received from Dick and his immediately throwing down the Sam card, there are some good reasons I have stayed with "adored." First, "adored" has the nice alliteration of being one of three As, as in "Appointed," "Accepted," and "Adored" Leader. That is nifty symmetry and kind of catchy, if you ask me. It's the triple-A of leadership!

Second, I too can pull a Sam card from the deck—"revered" is part of a group of words that includes adore, idealize, reverence, venerate, and worship. All of these words "refer to the warm respect and honor with which one may regard an admirable person or institution. Revere is less formal and less warm in tone . . . [and] *is more appropriate for an institution or idea than a person.* Adore suggests the most tenderness and warmth of any of these words."[1] So, with the implicit blessing of Sam, I am sticking with "adored." An Adored Leader is someone you regard with the utmost esteem, love, and respect; you honor them for both their achievements and their contribution to the well-being and satisfaction of others.

I don't know that I have quelled my critics, but there you have it: *an Adored Leader is one who is held close in our emotions because of their contribution to our well-being and satisfaction.* The Adored Leader is more than a person in charge; they are a part of our lives, to be remembered and cherished for their contribution to our personal success. My hope is that this book will provide you with the enthusiasm and grit to put yourself among the Adored Leaders as someone who makes the lives of others better than they otherwise would have been. The objective of this book is to put you on the path to contributing to the success of others, following a step-by-step process of personal growth.

LEADERSHIP AS I HAVE EXPERIENCED IT

I started my career as the owner-operator of a hamburger stand in Los Angeles, California. From there, I moved on to earning MBA and PhD degrees and a position on the faculty of Cornell University in Ithaca, New York. While I arrived on campus as a real green bean, I was also full of myself. I was arrogant and certain that I knew all that was worth knowing about organizations and their leaders. I was wrong; in fact, I was very wrong. It took me several large lumps and more than a few years to realize that I didn't know it all—or even most of it all.

Slowly, I came to realize that many of the leaders I worked with were really good teachers—if only I would open myself to what they had to teach. Along with this awakening, I came to understand that being a leader and being a teacher are two sides of the same coin in that you can't be good at one without being good at the other. "When the student is ready, the teacher will appear" is an old saying, and one that has a lot of personal meaning for me.

I was ready to learn, but learning can't be rushed, so it took a while for me to digest the lessons embodied in the words and behavior of my leader-teachers. I worked at it, but had no cosmic insights that propelled me forward. My growth was more like a slow layering of experience and an even slower realization of what that experience meant. One of the things that I was good at was understanding what I was experiencing. Today, we call it "putting things in context." I had a way of doing that, and it enabled me to learn a lot.

It was my habit to write down what I thought I had learned to see if it made sense. Often I literally drew pictures of the lessons learned, trying to understand what mattered or what caused something good or bad to happen. (Some of my favorite pictures are included in the following chapters.) As I distilled the lessons taught by my teachers over the years, I began to think in more concrete terms about three questions that intrigued me:

1. Why are there so few Adored Leaders?

2. Are there hard-and-fast principles that an accepted leader can follow in order to become an Adored Leader?

3. If so, how can these principles be taught?

These are three related questions, but in a chicken-and-egg sort of way. Nonetheless, they have caused me to search for a few immutable principles that could be distilled from my experience and study to be taught to leaders willing to do what it takes to grow to the next level. Equally important, I wondered if there were things embodied in what the bad leaders consistently do that should be avoided at all cost. Fortunately for the student that lives within me, it didn't matter whether a leader was appointed, accepted, or adored: each of them taught me valuable lessons that, hopefully, have accumulated over the years and that I share with you in the pages that follow.

I Am Not the Standard

I am a leader too. But I'm not an Adored Leader in the terms that I will describe in the following chapters. Despite having cofounded a company with a forty-year track record of success, I would put myself in the top 25 percent of the accepted group. Better than average, but not adored. My forte and zone of comfort have always been ideas and insights—sometimes inspirational—and untethered optimism. As I look back on my career, it seems to have helped a lot that I could find the humor in most situations.

I never really liked having to manage people, nor was I focused enough on the bottom line. I have liked almost all the people who have worked for our company over the years and have genuinely loved quite a few of them. Moreover, I am fascinated by people, the human spirit, and that thing we call grit—but I have an Achilles' heel: I don't love having to tell people what to do or having to keep track of whether they do it. Don't get me wrong: I'm not down on myself. I was a CEO for a very long time, and it was a time of growth and prosperity for our company. I know that I had something to do with that, but reflection tells me that the company would have been better off in the hands of my cofounder, Marta Erhard. Like a lot of leaders, I have 20/20 hindsight when a little more foresight would have gone a long way.

THREE THINGS ABOUT LEADING THAT MATTER

So here is the first lesson I learned. This one is mostly from the biographies and autobiographies I have read over the years about people who have left a mark on the world. Early on, I developed the habit of reading them as detailed leadership texts rather than as biographies or memoirs, trying to create a set of general principles in terms of the what, how, and why of leadership. So here goes—the first lesson is this: *Making a positive difference in the lives of others is the essence of leadership.*

The second lesson I learned is that the bright lights I have studied were *always* distinguished by two characteristics, namely, *achievement and human goodness.* These Adored Leaders not only achieved great things; they were good people to boot. What I concluded is that it was not achievement or human goodness alone that defined these leaders; rather, it was that their achievements *and* goodness were what drew others to them. Simply put, they were good people who achieved much in their lives and did much for others. As an aside for now, lest you think that Adored Leaders are faultless, that does not mean that they didn't have shortcomings. All of them did, and more than a few had big ones.

The third lesson may be the most important one: *none* of the Adored Leaders I knew or studied got to be that way by accident of nature. They were intentional, extraordinarily hardworking, smart enough, and chose a different path from the other accepted leaders of their time. *It was their intention to do better and that choice to be better that set them apart from accepted leaders, regardless of the context of their leadership.* Some were entrepreneurs, others were politicians or religious leaders, and still others had distinguished military careers—all of them knew how important it was to make their team members feel successful.

The fact that how good a leader becomes is a *choice* fits nicely with my general philosophy of life: *each of us is responsible for what we achieve and how we achieve it.* The big difference I have noticed is that some leaders have a head start on others. For example, Teddy Roosevelt's roots in extreme wealth, encouraging and enabling parents, and limitless opportunity contrast sharply with Abraham Lincoln's roots in extreme poverty, parental neglect and absence, and zero opportunity. The takeaway is this: *it does not matter where you start, only where you end.* Ultimately, it's up to you to decide how hard to work and where to apply your efforts.

The Starting Point of Personal Growth

The starting point is to answer an important question: *How good a leader do I want to be?* It's a serious question, as your answer will shape your destiny. As I look back on my experience working with other leaders, it's apparent to me that most leaders simply don't ask that question of themselves—at least, not in a way that makes them have to think hard about what they will do. I'm not shocked by this conclusion, as I never asked the question of myself either. Nonetheless, *it's a question that gets answered regardless of whether you formally ask it.* The inevitability of an answer caused me to dig even deeper into the memoirs and biographies of Adored Leaders to understand how they thought of themselves and what they did that was different from accepted leaders. In short, how did they separate themselves from the pack of accepted leaders?

What I saw was a pattern of choices that gave them an edge. In the chapters that follow, I'll identify these defining differences and outline what you need to know about them in order to make such differences your edge. The book, then, reveals the path from being an accepted leader to being an Adored Leader.

APPOINTED, ACCEPTED, AND ADORED ON D-DAY 1944

The triad of appointed, accepted, and Adored Leaders is one of the few insights that came to me in a flash. It was the result of studying Steven Ambrose's fascinating classic *Band of Brothers*, his history of World War II E Company, 101st Airborne Division. I read the book as a deep-dive into Richard Winters's personal journey from being a new college graduate just before the war, to being appointed a second lieutenant in the US Army, and, from there, to being adored by his soldiers:

> Winters came to the company as a recent graduate of Officer Candidate School. [One of his men described him as ensuring

that] "We fought as a team . . . like a machine . . . We were smart; there weren't many flashy heroics . . . getting the job done was more important . . . he was my total inspiration." [His regimental commander echoed this respect, saying:] "His personal bravery and battle knowledge [even in his first battle] held a crucial position when the going was really rough."[2]

Several years later, one of his men who stayed in the army and became a founding member of Delta Force wrote him a letter:

> You were blessed (some would say rewarded) with the uniform respect and admiration of 120 soldiers, essentially civilians in uniform, who would have followed you to certain death. I've been a soldier most of my adult life. In that time, I've met only a handful of great soldiers, and of that handful only half or less come from my WWII experience. . . . The rest of us were O.K. . . . good soldiers by-and-large, and a few were better than average. . . . I know as much about "Grace Under Pressure" as most men, and a lot more about it than some. You had it.

Later, in the wake of the 2001 HBO hit series *Band of Brothers*, Winters was asked what he thought it took to be a leader. His response, like his leadership, was humble, thoughtful, and detailed:

> You do your best every day. . . . My greatest satisfaction . . . came from knowing that I got the job done, that I kept the respect of my men. . . . For the nine months prior to the invasion [D-Day], I studied, developing my . . . perspective on command. . . . It was a chance for self-analysis. If you listen . . . you will find that your self-consciousness will tell you if you are getting off

track. Nobody will have to tell you. . . . If you . . . honestly look at yourself, you will be a better leader.[3]

His growth stood in stark contrast to the lack of growth of another officer in E Company. They were polar opposites—Lt. Richard Winters served his team, while Capt. Herbert Sobel served himself. As a result, he never grew beyond being an appointed leader. He owed his position to his rank rather than his contribution to his team's success. If it had not been for the stark contrast between Winters and Sobel, I likely would have missed the insight that there are three levels of leadership.

If you aspire to be an Adored Leader, it's critical for you to note that Winters did not somehow magically become adored. Instead, he recognized that he knew nothing about leading men in combat and, with clear intent, set out to master whatever there was to know about leading a combat platoon. He did that, and more—and, on his way, he passed through the first two levels of leadership to become an Adored Leader. His pattern of intentionally getting better and better is a hallmark of Adored Leaders like George Washington, Harriet Tubman, Abraham Lincoln, Teddy Roosevelt, George C. Marshall, Eleanor Roosevelt, and Indra Nooyi, to name a few.

YOU ARE WHAT YOU REPEATEDLY DO

Will Durant nailed the habit thing when he said, "We are what we repeatedly do. Excellence, then, is not a single act, but a habit." A leader who excels does so by practicing the habits of excellence. It's as simple as it sounds, but so very hard to do. If that were not the case, there would be no need for this book.

Habit formation is the process by which new behavior becomes automatic. Someone who instinctively reaches for a cup of coffee upon waking has a habit, and so does the person who automatically laces up her sneakers, leashes herself to an enthusiastic dog, and hits the street for an early morning run. However, one of the crummy things I've noticed about habits is that they can be hard to break. That seems to be especially true for bad habits. For example, it's always been easier for me to break the habit of lacing up my running shoes than to break a habit like grabbing a candy bar in the checkout line at the grocery store.

Habits—like grabbing a candy bar—are etched into our neural pathways by lots of grabs. That's why adding a new habit is difficult, because there is no pathway or picture to help us establish it. That's especially true when there is some pain involved in building the habit—think changing what you routinely eat, as an example. The further away the new behavior is from our familiar patterns of behavior, the harder it is to habituate. By my reckoning, Richard Winters worked very hard to build four habits on his journey from appointed to Adored Leader: *focus, preparation, commitment,* and *reflection*.

Focus is the first habit. Lewis Carroll summed up its value: "If you don't know where you are going, any road will get you there." Good point, but what is it that Adored Leaders focus on? First and foremost, they focus on the mission—that is, what is to be achieved. Winters wanted to be a good platoon leader, one who got the job done with a minimum of loss of life. Second, Adored Leaders focus on how it will be achieved. Winters "interviewed" more experienced officers in order to identify things to do and things to avoid doing. Third, they focus on building an effective team and keeping it effective through clear expectations and accountability. Winters had a good understanding of the strengths and weaknesses of his team members and assigned them tasks accordingly. Focus is the blocking and tackling of effective leadership for both accepted and Adored Leaders; however, among the latter, I have never known one that did not create and adhere to a disciplined approach to staying focused.

Preparation is the second habit. A leader who excels *practices the habits of excellence* described in the following chapters until they are an automatic part of his or her behavior. The caveat, of course, is that you have to know which habits to acquire and, just as important, which ones to break. There really is something to that "practice makes perfect" thing about which our teachers and coaches were quick to remind us.

Commitment is the third habit. This involves far more than being engaged; it's giving a part of yourself for the benefit of others, including your enterprise, team members, and community. When leaders study and work to develop the habits of excellence, they are spending a resource they can never replace—their time: time away from family, time away from relaxation, time devoted to being better. Commitment is sticking with something to make it better, especially after the glow of newness has faded. Followers may not be able to see your commitment, but they sure can feel it. Commitment was the driving force behind the legendary coach John Wooden's philosophy: "Success is mine when I work my hardest to become my best, and . . . I *alone* determine whether I have done so."[4]

Reflection is the fourth habit. There is no growth without reflection. Otherwise, you will stay in your comfort zone and stagnate, as the easiest path is to do what you have always done. Growth happens when you stop to think—reflect—and ask yourself: Is this my best? Is there a better way? What am I missing that is holding my team back? Why am I not achieving the intended result? Questions like these are the bedrock of personal growth because *growth does not come from experience, but from reflecting on the experience.*

Richard Winters thought a lot about his leadership and devoted considerable time to the study of military leaders, how they fought battles large and small, and how it was that they succeeded.

I have seen these habits and several others enough times to conclude that there is a pattern to leadership, especially Adored Leadership. This pattern brings to mind Leo Tolstoy's famous statement about families: "All happy families are alike; each unhappy family is unhappy in its own way." And I have seen a remarkable sameness to the Adored Leaders I have worked with that has led me to conclude that there are principles of leadership that can be used to move you from being an accepted leader to being an Adored Leader. The habits of leadership are the basis for your growth from where you are as a leader to being an Adored Leader, and the kind of leader your team needs you to be.

THE LEADERSHIP EDGE

An edge is something that provides an advantage in the pursuit of something valued. The Leadership Edge puts six different stepping-stones together to achieve one end: *being an Adored Leader* that creates your personal edge, starting with a definition of a leader and encouraging you to create one of your own. The stepping-stones summarize the leadership principles I have identified in a way that is easy to understand and use.

1. **Define** means to begin with the end in mind and answers the question "What is a leader?" I provide a definition, which you are free to use, or you can provide your own.

2. **Know** means to understand the driving force that underlies

positive relationships and what it is that an Adored Leader gifts to his or her followers.

3. **Be** is about developing your personal character—that is, how you approach the challenge of being a good person.

4. **Universal Promises** refers to what Adored Leaders promise their team members and what Adored Leaders expect in return.

5. **Measure** means monitoring your progress on your journey to being an Adored Leader.

6. **Achieve** is about the destination of honorable character and being an Adored Leader.

The late Stephen Covey was a good friend of mine and a significant influence on my understanding of leadership. We worked together for a number of years at a start-up called Steak & Ale back in the 1970s. It was there that Stephen worked to articulate and sharpen his now-famous *Seven Habits of Highly Effective People.*

I remember him working with a grease pencil and overhead projector (it was a long time ago!), sweat popping out on his shiny pate whenever he stumbled over a principle. It was obvious that he was teaching while simultaneously refining what he was teaching. Stephen was sharpening his principles in real time as he lectured the group, pausing to rephrase, revise, or reverse himself, and generally perfecting his thoughts. "Begin with the end in mind" is one of my favorites of Stephen's seven habits. It just makes so much sense that I'm going to start the discussion of the path to being an Adored Leader with a discussion of what an Adored Leader is—the end you have in mind. Doing so not only provides an opportunity to understand what an Adored Leader is, but, from that understanding, also allows you to decide if it's a journey you want to make.

The remaining nine chapters are stepping-stones on the path to being an Adored Leader that introduce you to each of the components of the Edge in detail, sufficient to get you started on your journey. As you dig into each of the chapters and see how easy the material is to master, hopefully you will want to make the journey.

The Head, Heart, and Hand Triangle

After reviewing this introduction to the book, a friend of mine asked me a really good question: "Can you teach someone to be an Adored Leader?" My answer was, "Not so much teach, as point in the right direction." It's that whole "when the student is ready, the teacher will appear" thing again. The nub of it all is that you have to intend to be an Adored Leader before you can be one, *and* you have to be willing to open your mind and do the hard work that it takes. The *Head, Heart, and Hand Triangle* is part of "when the student is ready" and is one of the pictures that I use to help leaders to understand the habit-building process and how to apply it to themselves.

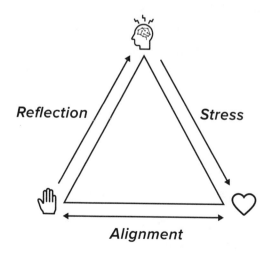

The head represents the knowledge and understanding of what it is that you intend to do. Its importance is illustrated by how often we start and stop new things, hit obstacles we did not anticipate, or begin actions that were more complicated than we expected. Using your head before your hands is often the key difference between success and failure.

The heart represents your emotions, values, energy, and what you will actually do. It has been my experience that people often go with their heart before understanding with their head what is required in order to be successful. Often, stress is the result of this disconnection. You can see it most easily in a job where you are asked to do things that you do not believe in, like upselling a customer who does not need or want to be upsold to a more expensive product or service. That can be a conflict between what you understand you are to do and what your values tell you is the right thing to do.

The hand represents action *aligned* with the power of knowledge (the head) and commitment (the heart). It is alignment that keeps you from wasting your time doing stuff that will not work. Finally, there is the feedback between your hands and your head. It's called "reflection," and this is where you think about what you have done in order to check its alignment with your heart and to discover how you could have done it better. You will find routine visits to your Head, Heart, and Hand Triangle to be invaluable on your journey to being an Adored Leader, but be forewarned: that is not what you are likely to do.

HARDWORKING IS NOT THE SAME AS HARD WORK

For the most part, the leaders I have known have been both hardworking and a mystery to me. One of the more perplexing things about them is how many of them have an almost prideful refusal to be students of the very thing they are paid to do: lead! I have been asked so many times to keep things "crayon simple" that I have run out of crayons. It's not that I don't like simple. I like simple as much as the next leader. At the same time, I know from experience that simplistic is a sure path to disaster.

Complexity is part of the human condition and, therefore, part of leadership. It's also the reason that professors routinely describe companies as "complex organizations." I'll go further than that: wherever more than one person is involved, complexity is inevitable. Everything seems to be interconnected; change this and you not only get a change in what you thought you were changing, but also a change in something you never anticipated changing. Often, leading can seem like plugging holes in a leaking dike.

You change the standards on who you hire in an effort to get better performance, but then employee turnover goes up. The very A-Players you insisted upon having are insisting upon your providing an A-Work Environment, or they quit. Go figure, but it makes perfect sense in that you can't introduce eagles to turkeys and expect the eagles to act like the turkeys. That's why employee turnover usually goes up when effective hiring procedures are introduced: people with higher standards set higher standards for others. Hence the law of complexity: you cannot change one standard without it affecting all related standards. The refusal of leaders to distinguish simple from simplistic is one explanation for the common practice of leadership by soundbite. I also think that it explains the lack of Adored Leaders in all walks of life—politics, business, military, education, media, and so on.

Think about it this way: What if your company's general counsel refused to stay current with the relevant case law or your controller failed to stay abreast of the changes in the general accounting rules? You'd jump up and down, and they would be gone in a minute. On a more personal level, what if your physician didn't bother to stay up to date with what's new and it could affect your health? Would you trust the doctor's judgment? Of course not.

There is a paradox: leaders typically work hard, and most of them have high standards, but, at the same time, many of them are intellectually lazy. This tendency to postpone their homework keeps them in a state of *willful ignorance*—that is, blowing off useful knowledge that is easily available and critical to their success. "Leaders who little know, little grow" is how Ben Franklin summarized the consequences of willful ignorance. He was right two hundred years ago, and he is right today.

Clearly, being a hardworking leader is not the same as doing the hard work of improving your knowledge of the profession, lining it up with who you are, and then executing it at a high level. Not doing the hard work of learning to lead at the highest achievable level has had serious consequences not only for the state of leadership in all sectors, but also for the people who trust them. This book is a small effort to change that state of leadership in as few pages as possible.

1

WHAT IS AN ADORED LEADER?

"I AM A LEADER BECAUSE . . ."

The beginning of wisdom is the definition of terms.
—SOCRATES

I looked it up: a leader is "one who leads or guides." That makes a lot of sense, but at the same time, it's not a very useful definition in that it won't put you on the path to being an Adored Leader, as it says nothing about how to lead or guide your team. So let's focus the definition a bit more by asking that it be *observable* (I know a leader when I see one because of what they are doing) and *measurable* (I know that leading has happened because I can point to the results).

How do you define a leader? It's a question I frequently ask the members of a leadership team when I first start working with them. I get many answers that I'm sure you are familiar with, such as "leaders are role models," or "leaders are coaches," or "someone who gets things done through others." These are not bad answers and are all true, as far as they go. Leaders do all of these things in the course of being one who leads or guides. But if you're working on improving your leadership skills, answers like these can be more frustrating than helpful. That's because they don't add to what you already know about leadership.

I dig a little deeper by asking the participants to write down their definition of a leader in one sentence. Then, after a few minutes, I say, "On the count of three, read your definition aloud." They do, and, of course, all you hear is the cacophony of people talking over one another, all saying something different. The noise prompts a few giggles, and it might seem unfair of me to do that when I know what I am going to hear won't be intelligible. But I do it to reinforce the insight Socrates had more than 2,500 years ago: "The beginning of wisdom is the definition of terms."

Without shared definitions of the things that are important to success, a team will not be on the same page, let alone in the same paragraph—and that's a problem. Just a few degrees of disagreement on important terms like *success, brand,* and *sales growth* will have major consequences for the people doing the day-to-day work of taking care of customers. While I usually work with the senior leadership team, each member of the team also has a team, and so on throughout the hierarchy of the company. That fact makes clarity an underappreciated leadership asset. The need for clarity is what Stephen Covey had in mind when he articulated his principle, "Begin with the end in mind." His point: *the clearer the destination, the more likely a successful journey.*

THE MAKE OR BREAK OF LEADERSHIP

Before we get to the definition of a leader, let's talk about what leaders are responsible for. One of the biggies is creating the right culture. Your team's culture—whether you have consciously created it or simply allowed it to exist—will make or break your effectiveness as a leader. This fact of success is what legendary management guru Peter Drucker had in mind when he said, "Culture eats strategy for breakfast." If you have ever tried to change the performance of a team, you may have learned that bit of wisdom the hard way. It is also why it's a good idea for you and your team to spend whatever time it takes to define the team's success and how it will be achieved, as doing so is tantamount to defining your team's culture.

If you share my belief that one of the primary responsibilities of a leader is to build a high-performance culture, then defining terms is much more than a team-building exercise; it's *the* critical step in getting the right culture in place. That's because language is a significant part of any culture. Let me explain—better yet, let me share my picture of the components of culture.

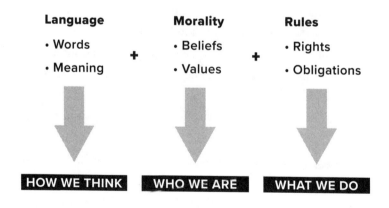

Language		**Morality**		**Rules**
• Words		• Beliefs		• Rights
• Meaning	**+**	• Values	**+**	• Obligations

HOW WE THINK	WHO WE ARE	WHAT WE DO

The Components of Culture

A culture is the shared beliefs about success and how it is achieved that guide the thinking and behavior of a group. This widely accepted definition of culture explains why culture-building is *the* major responsibility of a leader: the wrong culture guarantees failure, and the more wrong it is, the faster the failure. A culture in which beliefs about success are not widely shared or clearly understood is *always* plagued by conflict, bad feelings, and poor results.

Another reason for *intentionally* creating your team's culture is that your leadership creates a culture anyway. The question is whether it's the one that best serves the mission of your team. Anything less than a strong "Yes" to the question means that you have the wrong culture. So let's dig a bit deeper into culture in terms of its language, morality, and rules.

Language is how thoughts and ideas are transferred from one person to another. When someone asks, "What are you thinking?" it's impossible for you to answer without using language. Language—in all its forms—is fundamental to culture and the foundation of all human relationships. That's why the closer together people are in their use of the same words and understanding of the meaning of those words, the more effective the communication among them will be. An example from a friend of mine who runs a restaurant company illustrates the point. Restaurants need to be clean not only for customer safety, but also for those customers to want to return. But communicating to employees what "clean" means has always been a challenge. As my friend makes the point, "What my sons think is a clean bedroom is not even remotely close to what their mom thinks is a clean bedroom, and that's different still from what I think is a clean bedroom." So this friend uses the term "immaculate" instead of clean, as he finds that employees share a similar understanding of the word and its meaning. The point: the communication or transfer of what you're thinking to your team members, and vice versa, depends on shared understanding of words and what they mean.

Morality is a culture's guardrails, as it answers an important question: What is the right thing to do? A culture's right and wrong things to do are communicated through language but understood in terms of beliefs (things we hold to be true) and values (what we think it means to be a good person). It's differences in beliefs and values between one culture and another that makes it wrong to overcharge a customer in one culture, but not in another. For the former, the belief might be something along the lines of "honesty is the best policy" while the value might be "justice—do what is fair." What a culture's morality does is to lay out the boundaries of behavior by defining what will and will not be done in order to be successful. It's in the light of the function of morality that the arguments you hear today about wokeness, political correctness, and so forth should be understood as they amount to efforts to change the morality of a culture, and therefore to change the culture.

Rules tell people what they are entitled to as a member of the culture, as well as what they are obliged to do if they want to remain within the culture. The culture's *obligations* are what a leader communicates when she sets standards and expectations or holds a team member accountable for not meeting an obligation. And it is the culture's *rights* that are expressed when preference is given to promotion from within rather than to looking outside of the culture for candidates to fill jobs that have more responsibility and higher pay. It says that team members have the right to be rewarded for their contribution to the team's success by being promoted to a position of more responsibility and rewards. It's also recognition that old cultures are not built with new faces. The important lesson is this: the *only* way to change a culture is to change its language, morality, and rules. Intentionally or unintentionally, culture change is what happens when a company is sold and taken over by new leaders who have a different set of beliefs about success and how to make it happen. In my experience, the inevitability of this change is why many company founders prefer to be succeeded by internal ownership than to sell to external buyers. It's very unlikely that external buyers share the same beliefs about success and how it is achieved as the existing leaders of the company. There is no judgment of the beliefs of the new owners in this change; that comes with what happens in terms of how successful the changed company turns out to be.

An Adored Leader

It's harder to be an Adored Leader if you don't have a clear definition of leadership in mind. Equally important, it's almost impossible to develop leaders if you don't know what a leader is and does. That brings me back to the purpose of this chapter: *define a leader.* I'll end the suspense by defining an Adored Leader:

Someone who earns the active loyalty of team members and molds them into a high-performance team.

What I like about this definition—other than the fact that it's mine—is that it enables you to know an Adored Leader when you see one. I also like that a leader can self-measure whether she is truly adored by answering questions like the following:

- Does my team routinely achieve the intended results—that is, win?
- Do I make my team members feel like winners?
- Are my team members enthusiastic and committed?
- Do people want to be on my team?
- Is my team a good source of promotable people to lead other teams?

These are pretty easy questions to answer in concrete terms. What they reflect is a critical component of being an Adored Leader: the ability to *earn active loyalty and build a high-performance team.* This is a good time for you to write down your definition of a leader. You can use mine if you'd like, and I would be flattered if you did so, but if you have another one that you prefer, go with it. Just make sure that it's observable, measurable, and something you can teach.

ACTIVE LOYALTY

What some leaders call loyalty isn't loyalty at all. Even though some team members might look like they're loyal, they may be staying because it's easier than leaving, or they feel a sense of obligation, or they're stuck, but it's definitely not the kind of connection rooted in an emotional attachment to the team—one that compels enthusiasm and high performance. It's easier to see this distinction with a customer example than with a team member example, so I'll share with you my experience on a recent cross-country flight.

Perhaps I should have felt at ease when the captain assured me that the delay was for my own safety. I like staying alive, but would prefer that it not involve three hours in my seat while still at the gate. As an alternative to that I would have been okay with being allowed to stay alive in the gate area where I could stretch my legs. Despite the fact that I have traveled more than two million miles on this particular airline, there is no way that I would describe what I was feeling during my wait as loyalty.

I'm not proud of it, but I was in a snit about the dehumanizing way the airline treated its customers (okay, me). I started ruminating over my status as a frequent-flyer biggie (or FFB). The airline calls me a "loyal customer." To show the strong bond between us, it sent me an exclusive-looking card and a set of luggage tags to prove my loyalty. But neither of these things were a comfort to me, nor did they make me feel loved. They're nice, and I like being appreciated, but they weren't helping much as I sat in my seat grumbling to myself.

I wasn't feeling like an FFB or feeling appreciated; "herd animal" is closer to the truth. On the face of it, more than two million miles on the airline should qualify me as a loyal customer, but perhaps not. I have about the same number of miles on each of the airline's two primary competitors. More importantly, I do not go out of my way to travel on any one of the three. For me, the only thing that distinguishes one airline from the other is its color scheme.

It occurred to me that "going out of my way" is a crucial ingredient of any definition of loyalty. Think about the quote in the introduction to this book, in which one of the members of Richard Winters's team describes him as "blessed (some would say rewarded) with the uniform respect and admiration of 120 soldiers, essentially civilians in uniform, who would have followed you to certain death." Now, that's going out of your way! They were willing to give something of themselves—in fact, all of themselves—to the leader. That's loyalty—in fact, it's *active* loyalty—*volunteering your gifts of enthusiasm, commitment, and extraordinary performance for the benefit of the team.* That kind of loyalty cannot be bought with frequent-flyer points.

It's More Than Satisfaction

Here's the thing: *employee satisfaction is too low a bar when excitement is possible.* Active loyalty is about creating excitement among your team members by doing some of the things that are described in chapters 2, 3, and 4. An actively loyal team member goes out of his way to support the success of the team because he cares about the success of the leader and the team and wants to be part of it, even at a personal cost

It's this personal aspect of active loyalty that makes it something you can't buy or compel. Instead, it's something you have to earn through your words and actions. In a real sense, *active loyalty is a gift from your team to you.* That's why I like to think of actively loyal team members as *volunteers* in your success. What team members volunteer are their enthusiasm, commitment, best effort, and a good word or two on your behalf.

The difference between bought and earned loyalty is the difference between compliance and commitment. The first is something I have to do. The second is something I *want* to do. As my example of the airlines illustrates, economic loyalty can be bought, but only at a very high price and never at the cost of a true commitment, emotional commitment, or a genuine thank-you.

One of the things that makes active loyalty so valuable is that its cost is borne *solely* by the team member, and not the team leader. Team members pay the price of their loyalty when they voluntarily take on tasks without being asked, support one another, refer their friends to the team as a place to work, and do that extra something that blows a customer away.

The cost to them is real: it's the team member's time and effort, things that the team member can never replace. That's what makes it priceless! It's for this reason that my definition of an Adored Leader includes the notion of earning the active loyalty of team members, and why your definition should too. The roots of how to earn active loyalty are the subject of chapters 2 and 3.

LEADER TO-DO LIST

☐ Complete the answer: "I am a leader because . . ."

☐ Ensure that your answer is actionable and measurable.

☐ Identify three situations with respect to your team where your definition of a leader needs to be applied immediately.

2

THE HEART OF CONNECTING

THE EMOTIONS YOU LEAD

> I can't deny the fact that you like me.
> Right now, you like me!
> —SALLY FIELD

What were you thinking? You've rented a time capsule, only to have it plunk you down much earlier in time than your vacation plan called for. In fact, you're near the beginning of human history and very much alone smack-dab in the middle of nowhere. It's cold and dark, and in the movie version of your journey it's raining sideways—mixed with a little stinging sleet. Even though you're really, really hungry, that low growling noise you hear is not coming from your stomach, and it's not the cold rain that's sending a chill down your spine. Something has eyes on you as it crawls toward you from the shadows.

For the first time in your life, you are totally aware that your survival is up for grabs. Since the Navy Seal lifestyle is not for you, facing down the Grim Reaper has you trembling. You're definitely in a pickle and facing a fundamental fact of humanity: *we cannot make it alone*. No way, won't happen, get over it. You need help—and you need it now!

While evolution has made this fact part of our DNA, our ancestors learned it the hard way. Their dwindling numbers were a likely clue. Whenever one of them wandered off to be alone with his thoughts, more often than not, he didn't return. Sure, there were bits and pieces to remember him by, but that's not the same as sitting around the campfire, popping a cold one, and kibitzing about the day's adventures. Survival was iffy at best, in a world dominated by larger, stronger, and faster animals that loved people, but in a menu sort of way.

There were still other clues to our precarious state, like how fast the kids in the group hid behind their parents' legs whenever the alarm was sounded. It was just another lesson in "loners can't make it." All this threat despite that large and magnificently complex organ we were so proud of—our brain. It turns out that being able to think things through is not a game-changer in a face-off with the Big Nasties—unless they happened to be chess players.

Of course, playing games with their human neighbors was not what they had in mind. Besides the lack of social inclusiveness among the Big Nasties, there's a troubling fact that has always been a thorn in the side of human survival: our brain takes years to develop and, even then, it's no guarantee of success. After all, it's housed in a relatively weak chamber, and vulnerable. When even a small dog can outrun the fastest among us, survival demands a unique solution. That big brain of ours led us to the discovery of a formidable force against danger and darkness: *take on the Big*

Nasties together, and follow it up with a group hug, laughter, and a trendy dance around the campfire. We learned that belonging to a tribe matters. In fact, *belonging* is a very big deal, survival-wise.

WE ARE DRIVEN TO CONNECT

Survival is why the ability to connect with people is such an important skill. While I don't think the intensity of the need to be connected has changed, over the past decade or so it seems to have taken on heightened importance, driven by an addiction to social media. Despite the fact that it has proven to be a poor substitute for authentic personal connections, social media owes much of its popularity to our need to feel that we're part of the tribe and that we are missed when we are not there.

Adoration Feels Good, Even When It's Handheld

I had a taste of *cluster-connecting* when a friend of mine invited me to lecture his class of thirty or so college juniors. As we were waiting for the class to start, I noticed that many of them had their heads down. I thought to myself: "They're spiritually preparing themselves for the sterling lecture to come!" I was pumped—and wrong. Turns out that their heads were bowed in a full-court press to keep their connections alive! Yep: they were simply staying connected with friends via their handheld devices and wanted to beat the bell that signaled the beginning of class.

Barely masking my disappointment at not being the center of attention, I asked for a show of hands: "How many times per day do you check for messages?" To my surprise, the total number of times was approximately "countless." (To put a number to it, the latest research suggests an average of fifty-two times a day, or about three times per waking hour.[1]) I knew in a flash that *quantity* of connection had replaced *quality* of connection in their way of thinking. But that's wishful thinking on their part, as it's quality rather than quantity that matters in terms of having a genuine sense of belonging. Indeed, study after study reports that the more a person uses social media, the less connected he or she feels. *Only a quality connection addresses our need for affirmation that we have a place.* That's a fact that you can use to move yourself along the path to being an Adored Leader.

The irony of the press to substitute quantity for quality connecting is that each of us has the secret sauce to create quality connections built into our DNA. Properly applied—that is, in person—the sauce soothes our never-ending need to feel as though *we have a place.* As an Adored Leader, you can use your understanding of this need and its mechanics of civility and caring (chapter 5) to build energy-producing, high-quality relationships with your team.

Belonging and Significance in Perspective

Clearly, we humans need other humans and, equally, we need them to need us. We crave hellos, hugs, handshakes, smiles, conversations, and warm goodbyes—and the sense that we are missed when we are gone. There was a terrific book written way back in 1989 about this sort of thing that dealt with what the author called "third places"—barbershops, diners, general stores, pubs—places where we know everyone and everyone knows us.[2] These are physical places where neighbors run into one another unplanned, and thereby put a little happy dance in their day. It's this third place—not home, not work, but another place altogether—where good tribal stuff happens. When I was a kid, it was our local community recreation center. Today, it's things like Starbucks and fitness centers that fulfill this need.

As I edit this chapter, the world is well into a forced isolation due to the coronavirus pandemic. I don't know who comes up with these names, but it's called "shelter-in-place." Although most of the news is about the economic impact of the shutdown, the social and mental health impacts are just as concerning. That's huge. From a social perspective, the implication is profound: we are alone! During the lockdown, Americans largely abided by the directive to shelter-in-place, but after six weeks or so of being alone, people started to complain and break the rules a little, jonesing to see their friends and family in person. As countless studies of people forced to isolate (such as convicts in solitary confinement) show, people needed to get back to their "tribe." I am fortunate to live in an area where it is easy to get outdoors while preserving the recommended "social distance" of six feet. As time sheltering in place went on, I noticed that the "hellos" from my fellow hikers became a bit more vigorous as we circled one another. Now, many of them stop to chat—at a distance. What happened is that we were doing what we could to connect, to see a familiar face (and dog), and simply to talk, but we were not connected. We were connecting, but not connected. I don't do much with social media, but I suspect my hiking experience was a lot like social media—there is evidence of a connection, but no connection.

If the story of our kind ended with belonging, all would be well and good. You'd just need to develop "belonging programs," and you'd be up to your ears in happy campers. By the way, that's exactly what dictators and identity-politicians try to do. However, belonging is far from the whole story of human success: *we think about the future, and what we see scares the bejeebers out of us.* Unlike with virtually all other species, the fact of our eventual mortality weighs on us, but it does so mostly just below the level of awareness.

So, here's the science in a nutshell. Our inability to make it on our own gave rise to an innate and insatiable need: we are driven to *belong and to have our belonging be significant*. Hence, the importance of the *tribe* in some cultures and our enthusiasm for joining groups, respecting hierarchies, and working hard to fit in with the other members of our tribe. We do these things because it enhances the likelihood of our survival (literally, in what are often referred to as third-world countries) and prosperity (anywhere). We are joiners and need constant affirmation that we have been accepted by the group.

Our concern is not along the lines of "What am I going to wear tonight?" but more along the lines of "Will I be alive to wear it tonight?" In short, we live with a genetic pucker factor, as each of us knows at some level that we will eventually end.[3] Among all of God's creatures, we are the only one that contemplates its own demise. If we let it, this "dirt-to-dirt and ashes-to-ashes" ending will make us crazy. Literally.

Indeed, not being able to hold our mortality at bay is a common explanation for some of the more serious forms of mental illness. Because mental illness is not a tolerable outcome or socially acceptable, we construct a compelling parallel reality along the lines of "somehow the world would be less without me—big time." In a word, we are compelled to have feelings not only of belonging, but also that we have *significance*: we are motivated to matter and be valued by those around us, and to sense, at some level, that we would be missed big time if we were not here.

Advertising our significance to others is one explanation for why we buy cars that are way more expensive than what transportation needs could possibly justify; why we absolutely have to have new clothes, only to wear them a time or two; why we live in houses that go far beyond our need for shelter; and why we decorate ourselves with jewelry—the more expensive the better. We are on a lifelong quest for praise and affirmation of our worth. We do what we must do: *validate that the world would be less without us.* That, by the way, is a very good thing. It's also something that Adored Leaders understand and work to address among their team members in ways that are valued *by the team member.* While Adored Leaders seem to intuitively understand the need for belonging and significance, accepted leaders do not. If they did, they would do much more than they do to cultivate this invaluable—and mostly free—team asset.

"You Really Like Me!"

The philosopher-psychologist William James noted that everything about our humanity—*every thought, feeling, and action*—is an effort to affirm our self-esteem. One of the most moving demonstrations of that need took place more than thirty years ago when Sally Field exclaimed with exuberant joy on nationwide TV, "I can't deny the fact that you like me. Right now, you like me!" as she was awarded an Oscar for her performance in the 1984 film *Places in the Heart.* Some people were put off by her childlike animated expression of joy, but not me. I loved how she openly did what all children loudly do and that most adults quietly do: *seek affirmation that we belong and have significance,* and, in so doing, give a boost of energy to our self-esteem.

Self-esteem is one of the things that all leaders should understand in more than a superficial way, as doing so can be used to the benefit of their team, its members, and themselves. I'd go so far as to say that self-esteem is the tipping point of our lives. When we have it in proper measure, we feel successful *regardless* of our level of objective achievement. Lack it, and we can't experience feelings of success *regardless* of how much we achieve. Leadership should be a wellspring of team member self-esteem, but too often it has exactly the opposite effect.

So back to my central topic: *our unquenchable thirst for belonging and significance is a supremely valuable tool for successfully making your journey to being an Adored Leader.* Self-esteem serves to put a spin on and filter how we interpret communication from others and from our environment in order to validate or reject our sense of belonging and significance. (I give examples and strategies for this in chapter 3.) Belonging and significance are so important to your personal and leadership effectiveness that action-oriented definitions are called for.

BELONGING AND SIGNIFICANCE DEFINED

Belonging: Feeling welcomed as a natural part of the group, suitably placed within the group, and secure.

Significance: Having a place within the group valued by others and feeling that what you do and who you are is irreplaceable.

Take some time to reflect on these definitions. Ask yourself how well you are doing at reinforcing your team members' sense of belonging and significance—letting them know that *they have a place on the team and that they make a difference to the team's success.* Belonging and significance, by the way, are what you should be communicating when holding a team member accountable, welcoming a new member to your team, or publicly praising a team member's success. In my experience, an Adored Leader *consistently* affirms the sense of belonging and significance of her team members and, by so doing, takes a step toward earning their active loyalty.

Indra, the Letter Writer

One of the mistakes many leaders make is thinking that they have to go large when it comes to affirming a team member's sense of belonging and significance. Hence, lavish holiday parties, big bonuses, and promotions. These are nice, but they are not the only thing to do and likely not the things that matter the most to a team member. *Gratitude is among the things that matter most.* That's because it pays off twice: first, when you get that rush from having done something nice for someone, and second, when that someone says, "Thank you. I really appreciate what you've done for me." That's a rush too.

Indra Nooyi, former CEO of PepsiCo and a member of the *Forbes* list of the world's most powerful women, knows the value of gratitude and shares it in a beautiful way. She tells the story of visiting her mother in India: "When I got home and I sat in the living room; a stream of visitors and random people started to show up. They'd go to my mom and say, 'You did such a good job with your daughter. Compliments to you. She's a CEO.' But not a word to me."[4] Other than a perfunctory greeting, the visitors didn't speak to her at all. Nooyi realized that it was her parents who the guests saw as responsible for much of her success, and it was her parents who deserved the praise.

The experience must have made Nooyi think, as she goes on to say, "The parents of great leaders and employees rarely get recognition for their work. It occurred to me that I had never thanked the parents of my executives for the gift of their child to PepsiCo." After the trip, Nooyi sent notes to each member of her leadership team, sharing the story of her upbringing and the experience at her mother's home. But the story does not end there, as she sent a letter to the parents of the people on PepsiCo's leadership team, expressing her gratitude, saying, "Thank you for the gift of your child to our company."

The letters opened a floodgate of emotions. She received letters from the parents saying they were honored and telling her how they had shared the letters with their friends and family. It doesn't end there, as some of the executives told her that it was the best thing that had happened to their parents—and "the best thing that has happened to me." Each year, during her time as CEO, Nooyi wrote four hundred letters to the parents of PepsiCo's leaders in gratitude for their contribution.

When I first read the article about Nooyi's habit of gratitude, I had mixed feelings. It took me back to my childhood, when my teachers sent notes home for my parents to read. Those notes always put me on pins and needles, until I found out what they said. If it was a "Tommy did this wonderful thing" note, I was over the moon with delight and got lots of praise from my parents, and a second rush when my mom shared the note with her friends. After I thought about it for a while, it dawned on me: Indra Nooyi is doing what my teachers did, only it's all positive—and for adults.

As Marillyn Hewson (chairman and CEO of Lockheed Martin, Inc.) has made clear, "success flows from the hearts and minds of the men and women you lead. Rather than treating the people you lead as you'd like to be treated, treat them as they would like to be treated. Small gestures like opting for face-to-face meetings or sending personal notes can have an enormous impact on teams and their morale."[5] These leaders teach, in concrete terms, an incredibly valuable lesson. *No matter how old, experienced, seasoned, hardened, or whatever we are, the need for belonging and significance—genuinely addressed—has the power to lift all spirits.* And it's free for the giving!

WHAT TO DO

You might want to write some notes—not emails, but real notes that are on a piece of paper, have your signature on them, and that you have to send by snail mail. So much of the high-payoff actions are free to do: welcoming your team members to work, asking about their children or some special event in their lives, saying thank you for a job well done, and saying goodbye and thanking them again at the end of their shift. What if each of your relationships resulted in an enhanced sense of belonging and significance for the other person? What you would soon discover is what all Adored Leaders discover: *you, too, feel an enhanced sense of belonging and significance.*

Giving and getting belonging and significance creates a positive spiral that not only increases your fulfillment at work, but also enhances the success of your team. All it takes is awareness of this universal and unquenchable need, the intention to use it to your team's advantage, and the habit of acting on your intentions. When you make enhancing the belonging and significance of others a habit, you soon discover the value of *quality* of connections over *quantity* of connections and give real meaning to the old saying that it's the quality of the time spent rather than the quantity of time spent that matters.

To understand how feeling significant can influence business and financial results, think about the last time you met someone new who you felt was indifferent to you as a person. I'll bet your energy level took a dive. Now, think about the last few times you made major purchases. Think about ones where you were made to feel that your business was appreciated and valued. Now, think about ones where everything went well, except that you felt the salesperson was on autopilot. Autopilot is good for airplanes, but bad for people, and it's bad for building a high-performance team.

Ask yourself, "What is something I could do tomorrow that would add to my team's sense of belonging and significance?" Then, do it. Think about the power of these feelings for earning the active loyalty of your team members. Thinking about what to do, like leading, is not a talent; it's a skill that becomes better only with practice—lots of action and reflection on your actions.

If like most leaders you value this skill, I challenge you to do something about it. Most of us would say we'll think about it, ask for a checklist, or conclude that we already have the skill in abundance. While experience tells me that the vast majority of leaders are good people and would love to contribute to the well-being of others, it also tells me that most of them do not submit themselves to the discipline required to develop the skills of caring or thinking about the opportunities to apply them for the benefit of their team. That is the challenge of this chapter and the next.

LEADER TO-DO LIST

☐ Identify three no-cost opportunities to create a sense of belonging among your team members.

☐ Identify three no-cost opportunities to create a sense of significance among your team members.

3

CREATING THREE STATES OF MIND

"I WANT TO FEEL SUCCESSFUL!"

All journeys start with a single step,
except the really hard ones—they can be
two steps forward and one back, a stumble, two
more forward, and then another forward.

At the first squad meeting each season . . . I personally demonstrated how I wanted players to put on their socks each and every time. . . . I would then have the players carefully check with their fingers for any folds or creases in the sock, starting at the toes and sliding the hand along the side of and under the foot, smoothing the sock out as the fingers passed over it. I paid special attention to the heel. . . . I wanted it done conscientiously, not quickly or casually. I wanted absolutely no folds, wrinkles, or creases of any kind on the sock. . . . I would demonstrate for the players and have the players demonstrate for me. . . . This seems . . . trivial, but wrinkles, folds, and creases can cause blisters. Blisters interfere with performance. . . . Since there was a way to reduce blisters, something the player and I could control, it was our responsibility to do it. . . . Next, I'd instruct the players on how to lace and tie their shoes precisely one eyelet at a time and then tying them in a double knot. . . . An untied shoe . . . can be particularly troublesome if it happens during performance. . . . These . . . trivial matters, taken together and added to many, many other trivial details, build into something very big: namely, success. . . . You will find that success and attention to details, the smallest detail, go hand in hand. . . . *When you see a . . . champion . . . you can be very sure that you are looking at an individual who pays great attention to the perfection of minor details.*[1]

Who is this rattling on about socks? It's John Wooden, basketball player and coach whose "love of preparation and teamwork—perfectly executed" marked the greatest record in all of sports history. In a win-at-any-cost society, his perspective represents the pinnacle of Adored Leadership simply because it stresses the *process of competing* at the highest possible level. Get the process right, and you get the winning right.

This does not mean that winning was unimportant to Coach Wooden. Rather, it means that winning is only one of several possible consequences of perfectly executed teamwork and a perfectly prepared team. Proof of his approach is in the details of his personal and team success: Wooden was a three-time All-America player, the consensus best college player of his decade, and the only person to be voted into the College Basketball Hall of Fame both as a player and as a coach. His teams won ten NCAA National Championships and eighty-eight games in a row. Without question, he was an Adored Leader. As one of his players, Marques Johnson, said, Coach Wooden cared. What I think is remarkable is that in the coach's long career at UCLA, only two of his players failed to graduate from college. Now, that is some kind of winning record.

THE STATES OF MIND

You can see in the socks story how creating a strong sense of belonging and significance among team members will take you a long way down the path to being an Adored Leader. With that one lesson, Coach Wooden made it clear that every player made a difference in the team's winning or losing—not just the stars. By so doing, he set himself up for earning the active loyalty of the whole team. His approach makes abundant sense in that it serves our drive to feel part of something and that we matter. It also reflects a fact of staffing: we are drawn to leaders who do that for us. For these reasons, creating a strong sense of belonging and significance is a genuine biggie among your efforts to build a high-performance team. However, belonging and significance alone will not generate a winning record.

Becoming consistently high performance takes something more. It takes the fairy dust created by *three states of mind* among your team members: *confidence, competence,* and *pride.* Without these states, sustained performance is not possible. That's what Coach Wooden was doing with his sock lesson at the beginning of each season.

Another of his players, Keith Erickson, said that the sock exercise taught him what he could control. He said that another of the coach's lessons was to be well skilled with the basics. He said Coach Wooden would focus the first few days of practice on fundamentals such as passing and footwork, and then only after that would players be allowed to attempt a shot. Through these lessons, he was building the team's *confidence* in their skills and *pride* that the team did things differently and was better prepared than any team they played.

Adored Leaders have a way of making their team members feel as though they can get the job done. This is more than feeling good about themselves or feeling part of the team. It's about a sense of confidence, competence, and pride—and being ready to compete. It's what the military calls "esprit de corps" and is the unifying force of a team devoted to its mission and to one another. Esprit de corps literally means "spirit of the group." However, it seems to be much more common in elite military units, sports, and not-for-profit organizations than in business teams. Four factors explain this deficit: lack of clear direction, inadequate preparation, emphasizing individual stars over teamwork, and not keeping up with changes in what it takes to compete.

Teaching Confidence, Competence, and Pride in Team

Overcoming these hurdles requires you to have a theory of how to compete. That's the same as having a theory of success, which is exactly what culture-building is about! While still in high school, Coach Wooden defined success as "the peace of mind that comes from knowing that I did my best to be the best that I am capable of being."[2] A telling aspect of Wooden's theory was that he defined what success meant to him *before* he developed his theory of how to succeed through mastery of the basics of competition. In effect, what the coach did was to outline a culture of success and then recruit players who fit it. Creating your own theory of success— your key to effective competition—is something that I encourage you to do. What Wooden's theory did for him emotionally was enable him to consider a game a victory regardless of whether it was a win or a loss, if it represented *the very best effort of his team*.

His perspective on competition represents an important aspect of being an Adored Leader: *focus on getting team members fully prepared to perform at the highest level achievable.* This is an internal standard of excellence in that the focus is not on how good or how bad others might be, but on getting the best out of what you have to work with today. In addition, it does not mean that winning is unimportant, but only that winning is the consequence of perfectly prepared team members and perfectly executed teamwork. His focus was on instilling *his* definition of success into *each* member of the team and then teaching them to work together as a team. In this sense, defining success is not a participatory process of negotiation between the team and its leader, but the result of what the leader says it is.

The bottom line is that you're the leader, and it's the leader who defines and builds the team's culture. The building process requires that you create the three states of mind in your team members. *Confidence* comes from repeated lessons—how to put on your socks so you can compete without needless distraction. *Competence* comes from practicing to automatic execution to create a muscle memory of success—dribble and pass until it's automatic. *Pride* comes from your team playing the best that it can, being determined to win, and setting a high standard of teamwork—it's "we did our very best," with no excuses. Listening to speeches by Coach Wooden and watching interviews of his former players, it's clear that this is how the coach instilled confidence, competence, and pride in his teams. Being a big believer in the importance of clarity, I define the states of mind as follows:

- *Confidence* is believing that the leader, self, and other team members are skilled and motivated to win, knowing how personal performance serves the team, and believing that the leader will not waste the team's time and effort.

- *Competence* is feeling ready to compete based on disciplined practice, the leader's ongoing teaching and coaching, having useful feedback, and receiving recognition for effective performance.

- *Pride* is the self-respect, self-esteem, and spirit derived from personal excellence and team achievement.

Notice that there is nothing tangible about these states of mind, except in the behavior of the leader and responsiveness of the team members. General James Mattis describes a similar concept in his recent book *Call Sign Chaos: Learning to Lead.* He describes three fundamentals of leadership—Competence, Caring, and Conviction— and describes them as forming "a fundamental element—shaping the fighting spirit of your troops. Leadership means reaching the souls of your troops, instilling a sense of commitment and purpose in the face of challenges so severe that they cannot be put into words."[3] While the consequences are obviously not so dire for a nonmilitary team, the importance of your team's readiness to compete—its esprit de corps—is.

This chapter, along with chapter 2, sets you up for what you need to know about the inner workings of human motivation. Those motives are *to belong and be significant, to be part of the team and to have that part matter,* and *to contribute to the team's success.* When you understand the power of belonging and significance combined with the force of the three states of mind, you are getting close to being able to mold your team members into a high-performance team—but not quite. That next step is a soft one: understand the importance of being a good human being. Chapter 4 will refresh and challenge your thinking about the importance of human goodness to your success, while chapter 5 will help you conform to the first rule of leadership: don't be a jerk.

LEADER TO-DO LIST

☐ What are you doing that routinely raises your team's feelings of confidence, competence, and pride?

☐ Create a plan for improving your current actions going forward.

☐ Note in specific terms the difference in your team that you expect to see as a result of raising your team's feelings of confidence, competence, and pride.

4

BE GOOD

Being truthful is a lot easier than trying
to remember what you said when you weren't.

The good things that happen in this world are not random; they
are the result of someone's good intentions. In a beautiful
summary of the importance of good intentions to quality of life,
Steve Allen wrote the following:

> God . . . is quite content to leave the necessary work of improve-
> ment to His human agents. The Deity has never yet introduced
> into the human drama a hospital, orphanage, convent, church,
> synagogue, temple, cancer research institute, or any other help-
> ful social institution. He leaves that to the more compassionate
> of His creatures.[1]

These compassionate creatures are the individuals among us
who take it upon themselves to make a difference in the lives of others. In terms of our day-to-day lives, it's our leaders who make the
difference. Leaders touch us every day in big and small ways.
The best of them attach a passion for the well-being of their team
members to their words and actions.

As a personal example, when my partner and I started our company almost forty years ago, we defined success as *building a company that we are proud to have as part of our lives*. With an intention as personal and subjective as this, we had to think about what would make us proud. Was it making lots of money, growing to be a big company, or something else entirely? As my partner and I discussed our definition in the early years of the company, we put very little emphasis on its economic success or the size of the company.

Instead, we focused on creating a culture of which people would want to be a part, and we wanted the company to be recognized by its customers as a significant contributor to their success. We believed, and still do, that "soft things" like these intentions are a source of inspiration to the kind of people who would want to join our company. As is true for any strong culture, our company has not been a good fit for several people over the years—and that's been okay with us. If we could have one do-over, I think it would be to have worked on reaching a high level of business success—if only because profit is a powerful enabler of good things.

THE PRINCIPLE OF INTENT

Coach Wooden made the point better than I can: "Trivial matters, taken together and added to many, many other trivial details build into something very big: namely, success. Little things make big things."[2] That is certainly true for the details of leadership. In fact, leader effectiveness is all about details. The *Principle of Intent* is one of the more important of these details:

The intent behind an act is every bit as important as the act itself or the result achieved.

Good intentions are the source of good things, the foundation of a values-driven company, and the key to earning the privilege of being an Adored Leader. Good intentions are the driving force behind all three outcomes. General James Mattis's recent memoir makes this point abundantly clear. At several points in the book he speaks to the importance of clear intentions—what he calls "Commander's Intent" as a guiding force for performance.

Mattis feels so strongly about the power of intentions that he recommends putting them in writing and communicating them in detail. That's a good idea. Personally, I'm usually the first one who is confused by my intentions, and making them clear to me by writing them down can only help to make them clear to others. That's what the discipline of writing them down can do for you too. One of the things that I really like about what General Mattis does is how he takes intentions to a high level of detail. It's part of his belief that one of the primary responsibilities of the leader is to ensure that all team members are crystal clear with respect to the leader's intentions. In leader-speak, it's called "clear direction"— and *it is a difference-maker.*

When your good intentions are sharpened by the addition of clear direction, what you discover is that good intentions and clarity do not make a one-way street. When team members believe that their leader's intentions are good and that they include the team, they are likely to describe the leader as sincere, genuine, and real even when the team fails. On the other hand, when team members believe that their leader does not care about what happens to them, they are likely to describe the leader as selfish and simply going through the motions—even when the team performs well. There must be some sort of magic surrounding good intentions that pulls in the goodwill and energy of the team toward its leader. As an added bonus (as though one were needed), good intentions combined with clear direction enable team members to do their job without constant supervision.

There Is a Hitch

A while back, I read something that both fascinated and infuriated me. It was a book by Howard Gardner wherein the author writes that most people have what he calls "a five-year-old mind." What he describes is a level of human development he calls "conventional," saying that to go beyond this convention requires both intention *and* concerted action.[3] (Perhaps what infuriated me was the fact that by the time I read the book, I was way, way north of five years old and could really have used the insight much earlier.) His point, though, is a good one: we are born naked in all ways; we are, essentially, a blank slate that waits for the story of our growth as a person and the kind of person-leader we will be—*appointed, accepted,* or *adored*—to be written.

Conventional development rests on the fact that we have the values that we manifest for the rest of our lives by the time we are between five and seven years old, *unless we do something to develop beyond that level.* Like the accepted leader, most of us reach a level of "conventional" maturity. At that level we have good values, obey the law, do our part, vote when we can, care for our children, and perhaps do a little more, like coach kids' athletics. Even though that sounds pretty good, as life goes, it's a life that doesn't make a hole in the world—unless *we decide to go beyond it.* I think this is a good explanation for the preponderance of accepted leaders and the lack of Adored Leaders: most leaders get better and better at doing what they have always done, rather than learning new things so that they can do more things better and better.

Here's the catch: in order to grow, you have to put yourself on an intentional path, with full awareness of the experience, risk, and learning it takes to have honorable character—that is, to make a hole in the world. This is a choice that all leaders make, regardless of whether they are aware of having made it. In this sense, being of honorable character is never an accident but an intentional path we choose to take (or not).

What it takes to move from the conventional path of an accepted leader is the drive to be better and the willingness to learn, fail, and learn again on the path to learning what is better *and* actually makes a difference in the lives of others. This is the process of *personal growth*, shaped by the maxim of an honorable life: *to act as though you love, even in the presence of someone you find to be unlovable.* That is not easy to do.

THE BUILDING BLOCKS OF CHARACTER

This hard path to honorable character compels those who take it to do things that go beyond conventional morality, sometimes at great personal cost. I'm in awe of people who have taken the path. As I was writing this section, some of the younger team members in Corvirtus (a company founded by my partner Marta Erhard and me in 1985) encouraged me to "de-geezerize" the discussion by using modern examples of such people. I looked but couldn't find any to draw from. It's not that there are not people of character in this day and age, but it takes many years of contribution to build a track record and other people's reflections to reveal true human goodness. So I'll stick to the ones I'm sure about.

Harriet Tubman was a slave who escaped slavery and, instead of staying safely in the North, returned to the South to help hundreds of other slaves escape at enormous personal risk. But that was not enough for her: during the Civil War she served as a cook, nurse, spy, and combat leader. After the war, she worked tirelessly for the rest of her life to win the right to vote for women. That's a track record. Nelson Mandela was imprisoned in solitary confinement for nearly thirty years for leading the movement against apartheid in South Africa. That's a commitment. Abraham Lincoln, Mahatma Gandhi, and Martin Luther King Jr. paid the ultimate price for their devotion to peace, unity, and equal opportunity. That's a sacrifice. General George Marshall sacrificed his dream of leading soldiers in combat to devote his extraordinary organizational talents to the administration of World War II and to the rebuilding of Europe and Japan following the war. That's a patriot.

What is it about these people that makes them so different? Some of the things they have in common are humility, seeing a clear path to something that will make a difference in the lives of others, and determination. Without exception, they took full responsibility for their actions and willingly paid the price of their beliefs, as many of them did not live to benefit from their own success. In a real sense, people of honorable character act as though they love all humankind. What's easiest to see is their inner compass of core values that compels them to act in the interest of others. Rather than sucking energy, their acts of love create it. While being an Adored Leader does not require you to put your life on the line, it does require you to put yourself on the line in order to make a difference in the lives of others.

Personal Character and Behavior

The examples I have used are luminaries who led very public lives; obviously, that is not the case for the vast majority of people of honorable character. We simply do not hear their stories. While the people we revere often have a record of considerable accomplishment, just as often, they do not. Many of them were people we simply met along the way—a particularly impactful teacher, a friend, or a leader we were fortunate enough to have worked for. Achievement is about more than the magnitude of what is done; it's about the love that is behind it.

My father was one of these people. He was a gifted mechanic. He loved to tinker, invent, and build things. If he was making something new, he'd make two if he could, as he knew the first one was teaching him how to make the second one better. I remember a barbeque fire starter he made out of two Number 10 tomato cans when I was a small boy. It worked with a single piece of newspaper as a starter. Years later, I saw the identical thing being sold in stores everywhere. He also made a car seat for the family's small dog. He wanted Sparky to be able to see out of the car windows as they traveled about the country. He made it many years before I ever saw one in a pet shop.

He was always generous with his time and talents. If there was something to be fixed, people said, "Call Al. He'll know how to do it." Sometimes our driveway and backyard looked like a car repair shop. He fixed the neighbors' cars and volunteered his help to everyone in the neighborhood—build a fence, paint a house, clean up after a flood—never asking for or accepting a dime. He was the "bestie" to a neighbor's son who had Down syndrome. Paul would follow my dad around, talking the whole time. My dad would give Paul "important stuff" to work on, they'd talk, and have lunch together in the backyard. Paul's innocence and gentleness seemed to affect my dad. He felt very comfortable and relaxed with Paul, and Paul with my dad.

But it wasn't all roses for my dad, any more than it is for many other honorable people. My dad had a dark side. Like with so many of our neighbors, his service in World War II left him damaged with what's now called PTSD. He did not talk about what happened to him during the war; he had violent dreams that decreased in frequency over the years but nevertheless lasted for the remainder of his very long life. My mom had to sleep on the edge of their bed (she called it "out of firing range") for those times when he lashed out in his dreams. He'd get up and patrol the house in the middle of the night and never remember doing so. He also had an explosive temper—and you never knew what would set it off; he had extreme difficulty trusting others, a tendency to drink too much, and was also a committed pacifist. I learned that last bit when I came home from college and told him that I had applied for a Marine Corps officer training program. This was in the very early years of the Vietnam War and I thought he would be proud of my decision; instead, he went ballistic telling me that the war would be a stupid waste of lives. Fortunately for our relationship, it turned out that I was not medically qualified for the program.

In any event, it took me well into my adult years to accept his dark side. My graduate work in psychology was a big help in understanding and accepting what had happened to him and how it had affected who he was. Only later did I conclude that he was also an example of what you see in many people of honorable character: a mix of contradictions, sometimes very big ones—and not all of them pleasant.

On his bright days—and there were many—he had a contagious zest for life, unbelievable physical energy, a generous spirit, a good sense of humor, and high standards. Good days or bad days, his word was his bond. From what my mom and his old friends told me about him, these qualities were who he really was. I concluded that the darkness he experienced was the price he and millions of others paid for their service in the war.

The lessons my dad's life taught me about character is something I could never have learned from books: intentions matter, the will to goodness matters, and that failure is inevitable. My dad was who he was, and, much later in his life, when he would finally talk about it, I came to realize that his dark side was a source of considerable sadness and shame to him. That mattered, too, as a context for his good intentions, as well as a way to accept his dark side and how our family experienced it. It is clear to me that none of us, including people of sterling character, get through life without some scratches and dents.

The Honor Pyramid

There is no mystery to being a person of honor or why it is that personal honor is the core to being an Adored Leader. The *Honor Pyramid* represents the sources of personal honor in three aspects of an Adored Leader's behavior.

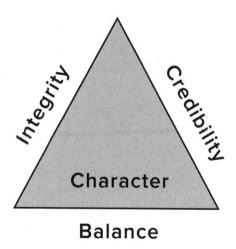

Components of Character

Competence and human goodness are the essence of character and have their source in three important behavioral habits: *integrity, credibility,* and *balance.*

Integrity is much more than many of us would like it to be. It's the pinnacle of self-awareness of your commitment to personal honesty. I think that Shakespeare's "to thine own self be true" summarizes it best, though I admit that "walking your talk" sounds sexier. What integrity represents is the perfect alignment of values, thoughts, and actions, as demonstrated by its three standards:

1. Make a clear decision about what is right and what is wrong.

2. Act on what you believe is right.

3. Pay the price of your actions.[4]

It's number three that takes down many leaders who claim to have integrity. When called upon to pay the price of their talk, they walk away from their talk and toward an excuse. The point: paying the price of your integrity is not negotiable, no matter how much you might like it to be otherwise.

Because integrity does not include any notion of competence, I pair it with the ideal of credibility. *Credibility* adds the force of *personal competence,* or *getting the job done.* This add-on is particularly important to the Adored Leader, as it gives weight to *every* leader's unsaid promise to team members: "Trust me. I'll get us there."

Balance leverages the *steadfastness* of integrity and the *competence* of credibility to be inclusive of everyone. Balance demands that you serve the interest of all stakeholders without favoring the interest of one over another. In this sense, balance is the arbiter of impartiality; it's a matter of speaking and acting in the interests of all. I like to think about it as a long-term boundary on the behavior of the Adored Leader.

Anne Wojcicki (cofounder and CEO of 23andme) put it this way. "I think that the most important things I can do as a leader are to be accessible and to be real."[5] Being truthful and being yourself is a lot easier than trying to remember what you said the last time you weren't truthful and real. While I don't believe there is such a thing as complete transparency, I believe that being open and clear about who you are is possible. Besides, I'm pretty sure that complete transparency is not a good thing for the relationships among people; better to, as Jordan Peterson would have it, "Tell the truth, or at least don't lie."[6]

BEING IN CHARACTER

As the quote from Will Durant in the introduction made clear, personal excellence is developed in the same way that any other positive habit is developed: namely, through disciplined practice. Practice, practice, and practice more, until you get it right. In my view, the disciplines of character center on one thing: the habit of *treating people as though they are loved.*

How character is developed is clear.[7] You simply have to do the heavy lifting of stating your intentions, clarifying them in writing, and practicing them until they become part of you. There is no shortcut or one-page version of this journey. You make it all, or you make none of it. Perhaps that's another reason there are so few Adored Leaders. The bottom line of character is that the more you practice acts of love toward others and especially those you find unlovable, the more natural the acts become until, finally, you no longer act as though you love; you *do* love. To quote Muhammed Ali: "To be great, you must believe you are. If you aren't, pretend you are until you are."

Character reveals itself in many ways. Former British prime minister Margaret Thatcher was not universally liked, but she was widely admired for her unstinting character. She made clear her intentions and what she stood for and what she would not stand for (integrity). She was a skilled and informed politician (credibility). Moreover, she had the courage to stick with her beliefs despite frequent and difficult challenges to her positions and brutal personal attacks both from within and outside her party (balance). She never backed down from a position that she thought was right, no matter how expedient or easy it would have been to take another course. She *was* her values, and thereby inspired her admirers and earned the grudging respect of her detractors. You really can't ask for more than that, as the loftier your intentions, the bigger target you will become.

The gist of what is demanded of you on your path to being an Adored Leader is this: *you have to love the people you serve at least as much as you love yourself.* If you are a leader driven to be adored, this is a matter of understanding what you truly value and then intentionally making it happen. Along the way, you will find that one of the indispensable aids to your personal growth is as old-fashioned and traditional as anything in the history of humankind. That aid is good manners, the subject of chapter 5.

LEADER TO-DO LIST

☐ What do you specifically intend for your team to experience as a result of your leadership?

☐ How will you know that you are delivering the experience you intend to deliver?

☐ What challenges do you face that could jeopardize your character in terms of your integrity, credibility, or balance? Be specific.

☐ What will you do about these challenges in order to avoid a compromise to your character?

5

BE CIVIL

One of the most underrated skills in business
right now is being nice. Nice sells.
—MARK CUBAN

A t all times, you have the opportunity to use two of the most
powerful relationship-building tools imaginable: namely, grace
and gratitude. The powers of grace and gratitude to cause good things
to happen are woefully underappreciated. These core muscles in the
chemistry of human connection seem to be less and less exercised as
time goes by. While I'm not sure why that's true, I'm sure that it is
true. If you think that civility is a trivial topic for a leadership book,
it's likely that you don't understand the power of good manners. The
opposite of good manners is not bad manners; rather, it is meanness
and denial of our worth as a person.

That's why the *First Rule of Leadership* (and life) is "Be nice, or,
at least, don't be a jerk." You see this rule broken all the time in
public discourse, and likely in private on a regular basis. It's usually
the same things: talking over one another, name-calling, accusa-
tion without fact, personal insult, lying, deflecting accountability,
closed-mindedness. These are symptoms of leaders being jerks.

We follow our leaders, and, as a society, we are following them toward being increasingly mean-spirited, rude, and self-centered, coupled with a resistance to be held accountable for it.[1] Indeed, we have leaders who appear to take pride in their boorish behavior and false accusations, others who hold those who disagree with them in contempt, and still others who feel no obligation to directly answer the questions asked of them. While that's just plain rude, it's also bad leadership.

As a result, we have testy campus protesters who clamor for "safe spaces" to protect themselves from the "microaggression" du jour; ironically, they often do so by denying a safe space to others if the "other" is there to present an opposing point of view. Then there are the ongoing public debates about important issues such as climate change, immigration, and abortion, with each side talking past the other, making no effort to understand and to be understood or to be well-informed. This behavior represents the decline of civility, a decline that discourages openness and saps the energy from people. It's also the least effective way to lead, hands down.

HEAR ME OUT—OR NOT

None of this is new to you or to me. I had been thinking about the state of American civility and social ineffectiveness when I was invited to speak to a group of second-year MBA students at a major university. The course was titled "Principled Leadership for Business and Society." At any time—but especially given the current times—that's an on-target topic for a course. It's also a subject that I know something about, so I was looking forward to sharing what I knew with the students.

According to the syllabus, one of the questions the course answers is along the lines of *What inclines us to follow some people and not others?* Given the title of the course, an implicit assumption is that positive or principled leadership is a real plus. Although no one told me what the principles being taught were, I guessed that one of them had to do with leader decorum. After all, there's not a big market for loudmouthed, rude, and tyrannical leaders. I think it's fair to conclude that negative leaders find it difficult to *earn* the active loyalty of their team members, which means they are also incapable of building an *enduringly* high-performance team. Finally, from a social justice perspective, leader manners are important because of the power differential between a leader and team members.

I accepted the speaking invitation with considerable enthusiasm and looked forward to interacting with students interested in the cornerstones of positive relationships and honorable character. From what the professors told me, the students were heavy on theory and light on practice. In a course aimed at teaching values, ethics, and morality to budding leaders, the students hadn't learned the *first* ingredient of a principled life: being polite at all times.

Excuse Me, but I Need to "See" What You're Saying

I told the professors before the class that I am severely hearing impaired and needed to be near the audience. (People with normal hearing typically do not understand that there is more to accommodating impaired hearing than turning up the volume. In my case, it's about clear and *close* diction that allows me to "see" what is being said, as distance dissipates sound clarity and my ability to combine lip-reading with the sounds I can hear.)

It was a large lecture hall, as two professors had combined sections of the class. From my teaching days I recalled large lecture halls filling up from back to front, so I wasn't surprised that this one was as well. What would have helped—and been an act of good manners—was for the professors to instruct the students to sit near the front out of respect for the guest speaker.

Students do not automatically sit in the front, so in a class meant to teach the value of virtue, it was up to the teachers to impose the "because I said so" rule. Small or trivial details like this set the stage and the standard for a team, whether it's a team of students or any other kind of team. In my teaching days, I would have told the students to be on time and to sit at the front of the class. It's been a while since I have had any students, but when I was teaching it's quite possible that I would have told them that I would "ding" them if they were late to a class when a guest lecturer was teaching. By not doing so, the professors missed an easy opportunity to shape the principles of the leaders they were teaching. Especially in the instance of teaching values, "because I said so" is a necessary tool of any teacher. Why else would parents use the tool so often? Because it works.

As I began the lecture, I set the students up for an easy show of politeness by telling them in a nice way (and, if I do say so myself, with some humor) about my hearing difficulty. I told them something like, "I hear your words, just not the ones you wanted me to hear." I ended up having to deal with an uncomfortable social gulf by scampering around the classroom in order to see what the students were saying.

While I was well prepared for the class, I had the impression that my talk had not been as well received as I would have liked, but I'll never know. Since the students were required to evaluate guest speakers, it would have been nice to have had my impression confirmed by a thumbs-down or corrected by rave reviews. This, of course, was bad manners on the part of the professors rather than the students, as I had asked to see the evaluations but did not receive them.

There is a piece of leadership that fits nicely here, and it is this: whenever possible, ask for feedback from your team members. The more you have, the more effective you will become. Finally, since I chose to give the talk gratis (though an honorarium had been offered), a thank-you note—or even a thank-you email—from the professors would have been an act of good manners on their part. So much for teachers as role models.

POLITENESS IS THE MOTHER OF VIRTUE

Politeness is a critical first step on the path to moral development.[2] Morality, at first, is totally an act—it's your parents telling you to "Say 'sir' and 'ma'am'! Why? Because I say so." *Politeness* ("One doesn't do that") is not an automatic act; instead, it's an acquired skill and one that comes before *morality* ("One shouldn't do that"). First, through the insistence of your teachers (your parents, your situation), it is a behavior that is all fluff and practice. From there, it becomes intentional, habitual behavior.

Politeness is a soothing virtue and a prime lubricant of positive relationships. *Politeness, or good manners (as my mom called them), is a choice to show respect and to protect the dignity of another.* This definition makes it hard to understand why anyone would choose to have bad manners, especially when a positive relationship would mean better results all around. Think about the last time you welcomed a new team member to your team. What did you do to put the team member at ease or to give them their first sense of belonging and significance?

Is Politeness So Hard to Do?

Nonetheless, bad manners are not only increasing, but also increasingly accepted. I have wondered why this shift downward in personal decorum bothers me so much. After all, I've just said that it's a contrived virtue—one that is made up and totally fake! For this reason, manners don't tell you much about a person one way or another. But they matter far more than you might think.

The influential writer Robert A. Heinlein concluded that "*a dying culture invariably exhibits personal rudeness.*"[3] Whoa! There is truth behind his observation, as researchers have found that small acts of rudeness can easily escalate to increasingly harmful events.[4] "I'm rude to this bastard, so why not lie as well?"—and so on, goes the escalation of destructive behavior. If you are still reading this book, however, you are likely to be leaning toward taking the journey to being an Adored Leader. If so, then part of that journey is learning how to earn the active loyalty of team members and mold them into a high-performance team. I can't see how bad manners could possibly aid your task. In fact, if your team members are A-Players, bad manners amount to shooting yourself in the foot in terms of team member turnover.

I have been called upon several times to work with leadership teams in crisis. One of the things that I almost always find is that the leader of the team has bad manners. I am not talking about shouting or throwing things so much; rather, it's tons of little stuff, like chronically being late for meetings, rescheduling meetings, monitoring their iPhone during meetings, being unprepared for the meeting, talking over team members, demeaning ideas that are not their own, and generally being a jerk, which sucks the energy out of the team. Bad manners are hard to ignore, especially when the team is under stress. While good manners may be overlooked, bad manners never are.

"You Like Me?"

The question mark says all there is to say about the morality of good manners. Being polite is not moral or immoral; it's amoral, neither confirming nor disconfirming the goodness of anybody. That's also why my classroom experience is a useful example: the students showed up, and I did my job the best that I could do it.

No one had bad intentions, useful information was exchanged, and life goes on. In short, in the scheme of things—the students' lives and my life—the class was of little consequence, except for being a perfect learning platform for an often-overlooked virtue: being *a person who is easy to be with.* That is the single largest hurdle that rude leaders have to overcome. Even when they have good ideas and their direction is solid, people don't want to follow them. Why? Because it's draining, instead of being a fulfilling experience.

The importance of politeness is the choice to appear to be better than we might really be. That's its lubricating value. The purpose of being polite is as simple as it is important to a leader's effectiveness: *to put people at ease and, therefore, make them more approachable, less defensive, and easier to deal with.* In this sense, good manners are a crucial first step to setting the table for better and more genuine things to come. Bad manners do nothing except tap into that uniquely human vice we experience as meanness and its consequences: intimidation, disregard, and shaming. That kind of behavior has no place in the toolbox of a leader.

FOUR (MAYBE FIVE) GOOD MANNERS

We come into this world innocent of all things—how to survive, how to grow as a person, and how to live a life that makes a difference in the lives of others. We are born in a state of total dependence, not only for our survival but also for our growth to becoming a contributing human being. We depend on our parents and early childhood experiences to teach us the values that differentiate right from wrong, but it's up to us to change the values we don't like in order to replace them with the ones that we admire.

That's a lot of responsibility, but it's also an empowering piece of information: you are not stuck! *All virtue is learned through education and experience and perfected through intentional practice.* Politeness sets us up to learn the disciplines of much more challenging virtues, such as courage, justice, and humanity. Politeness is in effect our training wheels for a values-based life. It's no more than acting as though you care until you actually do care. That is no more fake than Muhammad Ali's earlier comment "act as though you are, until you are." It's that whole habit thing again.

Being a principled or values-based person is an act of discipline before it is an act of habit. Of all of the virtues, politeness may be the easiest one to learn. In addition, it sets the pattern for learning other virtues. Which brings me full turn to my fixation on leadership and answers one of the questions posed by the leadership class: *What inclines us to follow some people and not to follow others?* I am convinced that good manners are part of influence, and, because they are part of making a good first impression, they are not a small part.

Thank You, Dr. Gaylin

So, what are the manners of an Adored Leader? I think I know or, more accurately, the late psychiatrist Willard Gaylin knew. It's been almost forty years, but I remember it like it were yesterday: I was reading Dr. Gaylin's book about feelings—that is, how we experience (feel) emotions like joy, envy, anger, and hope. It wasn't even part of the larger point he was making about feelings, but the good doctor referred to four modes of behavior—*respect, understanding, caring,* and *fairness*—that he saw as the qualities of a positive relationship. It was an "aha moment" for me. I immediately understood them as *the cornerstones of all positive relationships.*

One of the things that cemented my conclusion was to recast the four cornerstones in a negative sense: What explains the negative relationships I have been part of? Inevitably, I was able to see that I did not feel respected, understood, cared for, or treated fairly. And when the damage to the relationship was my fault, I could see how the other person could feel that I fell short in terms of showing respect, understanding, caring, and fairness. Had I known, I likely could have saved some relationships that were important to me.

I thought about the cornerstones some more, wrestled with how to define them and how to teach them, and wondered whether there were more. The latter thoughts brought me to the conclusion that "fun" should be added to the mix, not so much because it is necessary for keeping a relationship on an even keel, but because it brings the bounty of energy and renewal with it to lubricate the wheels of getting along in this world. So I defined the "Big Five":

1. **Respect:** showing high regard for the rights, values, and dignity of a person

2. **Understanding:** seeing things from the perspective of the other person without requiring that it agree with my own

3. **Caring:** being kind and thoughtful and behaving in ways that enhance the comfort and well-being of others

4. **Fairness:** working with a person in ways that are reasonable, open, and just

5. **Fun:** lifting the spirits of others through laughter, sharing, and celebrating success

You won't know if the Big Five work for you until you give them some thought and a test-drive or two. I recommend that you test-drive them by applying them to some of your important current relationships and asking yourself, "Am I being respectful, understanding, caring, fair, and fun?" If not, ask yourself (or the other party) how you could improve.

As you practice these elements with your team, remember to give yourself time to get good at them. Also, keep in mind that *good manners are an act before they are a habit, and a habit before they are you.* It's the skill of convincing people that you care about their comfort and well-being, regardless of whether you actually do care about their comfort and well-being. Even a faked smile is still a smile if it is faked well. In my experience, good leaders are good actors. Start acting! Feign interest in the comments of someone, even when a root canal would be a preferred way of spending your time; show interest when you have none; and generally put people at ease, when what you really want to do is to pound them on the head.

Before you go ballistic on me about the whole authenticity thing, it's the wrong argument. There is no faking when it comes to good manners: you are well-mannered or you are not, and, in the nature of this virtue, it does not matter whether you have to fake it. What matters from a leadership perspective is that good manners pave the way for what every leader needs to be able to do: earn the respect, understanding, caring, and fairness of team members—and on the good days, have some fun.

LEADER TO-DO LIST

☐ List three opportunities to build the cornerstones of a positive relationship into how your team functions.

☐ Implement one of the opportunities and then pay particular attention to how your team members respond.

☐ Identify an opportunity to discuss the cornerstones with your team.

6

DO KEEP
YOUR PROMISES

As far as A-Players are concerned,
you're always on probation!

Before my teaching days, there were my hamburger days. After graduating from college, I spent a couple of years working for a huge oil company. I hated the job, the bureaucracy, and the constant pressure to sell petroleum products to the dealers in my area, whether they needed them or not. I learned a lot from that experience, but the main lesson was that I don't like rules all that much. I'm also not so good at reporting to others. In short, I'm a bit selfish.

The experience and insights brought me to Jack in the Box as what was then called an "operator-lessee." It was the only way I could afford to "own" my own business, but it was the hardest work I have ever done. My first store was in Inglewood, California, a suburb of Los Angeles and right next to another burb called Watts. When I opened my "Jack" in the spring of 1965, staffing was not a problem. It was a low-income area with plenty of teenagers eager to work, even though most of them did not have a concept of what it meant to have a job in terms of showing up on time, having good personal hygiene, or being ready to work. It was an eye-opener for me, in that I had to teach them the discipline of having a job.

Like a lot of beginner entrepreneurs, I was seriously under-capitalized, so I did what others have always done: worked lots of hours. During the first year, I opened and closed the store most days. I had two days off, but that was only because we were closed on Thanksgiving and Christmas. My dream of opening the doors and being swarmed with a steady stream of customers did not happen. Instead, we had to build the business one customer at a time. Jack was an unknown brand at the time, so friendly service, product quality, and Jack's Secret Sauce were something we had to introduce to our customers.

It didn't help that I knew nothing about hiring people or managing them. My only leadership experience was as a safety patrol leader in grade school and a patrol leader in Boy Scouts and Explorer Scouts. It was not much of a track record, but it was all I had going in. I made many hiring, training, and management mistakes.

My failures made me think a little harder about who I hired. The first thing that occurred to me was to hire only the people who showed up on time for the interview and who were neatly dressed. I was learning from my problems but I still did not have all the answers, as I made plenty of mistakes. My staff and I plugged along, and the business slowly picked up steam. We even started to have some regular customers!

Then August 1965 happened. That summer, the Watts riots put my Jack in a ditch. As I recall, my sales fell by about 70 percent. People were afraid to go out, and those who did often came through the drive-through with a gun on the front seat. It didn't matter if they were black or white; they were afraid. In addition, many of the parents of my team members would no longer let their kids work nights. That wasn't all that bad, as there was a curfew. In retrospect, it was a hard time for all—my team, the parents, me, and my family. But things settled down and sales started to slowly pick up a few months later.

On the bright side, what I learned from this experience was that I liked to teach. I am sure that I was not very good at it in the beginning, but I liked seeing my team members grow. It was great when a team member started showing up on time and asking for more responsibility. I also appreciated that the restaurant industry then, as it is now, was a wide-open path to the middle class for those who didn't go to college. Like a lot of vocations, it's not rocket science. All you have to do is use your head, listen, love taking care of people, and be willing to work hard.

However, I was restless and eager to do something else. By that time I could take a bit of time to think, as I no longer had to open and close most days. I decided to go back to school. I started by earning an MBA degree and then surprised myself by earning a PhD as well so that I could teach at the university level.

Later, I reflected back on my time with Jack in the Box from a perspective of considerably more education and experience and concluded that I had done what Coach Wooden did: I did the best that I could—and I didn't suck. Mostly, I was pretty good after I got the hang of things. More importantly, my working, teaching, and consulting experiences led me to conclude three things:

1. All leaders want the same thing from employees, regardless of industry.

2. All employees want the same thing from leaders, regardless of industry.

3. All good teams are the same in terms of how they are good, regardless of industry.

That may not seem like much, but it's quite a lot because, by this time, I was looking to develop a formula for leadership success, one that could be easily taught and learned. In this chapter I'll briefly touch on what leaders want, but I will focus on what team members want that only Adored Leaders provide.

WHAT LEADERS WANT

I want team members who show up on time and are ready to work hard and, well, look for ways to contribute, support other team members, speak well of the company and their leader, recommend the company to other good people as a place to work, stay, and grow. That's it; nothing more! In a nutshell, these are team members you trust to do what you hired them to do. It's heaven. You can sit back, put your feet up, and pop a cold one, just as our ancestors wanted to do.

Whether at Jack in the Box or later at Corvirtus, this luxury was made possible by the presence of quality team members. At Corvirtus we've had numerous quality team members over the years, so I have had the good fortune to be able to enjoy lots of cold ones too. But we are in unprecedented times: before the coronavirus pandemic, we were at full employment, and there are hints as the economy begins to revive that we will get there again. What this will mean is that anyone who wants a job can find one. That's a whole different ball game. With a smoking-hot economy, high employee turnover, and an increasingly demanding workforce, how do you put yourself into a position to routinely pop a cold one?

GIVE TO GET

After *don't be a jerk*, the second law of leadership ought to be *give to get*. By that, I mean in order to get What Leaders Want, you have to give What Team Members Want *first*. It's in the bright light of this second law that I have always thought the practice of probationary employees was not a very smart thing to do. As I write this paragraph, it's February 2020 and the unemployment rate is at a sixty-year low. In some industries, such as hospitality, health care, and retail, it's effectively zero. That means zip, zilch—there are no unemployed workers who want to be employed. But my rant on probationary employees has little to do with this fact and more to do with the reality of A-Players: *they have always have a zero-unemployment rate as they can, and always could, easily get another job—no sweat*. Moreover, A-Players are the primo sources of What Leaders Want. That's why it's actually you who is on probation.

How Active Loyalty Works

It takes A-Players to consistently deliver a best-in-class customer experience. Without realizing it, the leaders in all service-intensive industries have implicitly assumed that A-Players are born and not made. That's no more true than the belief that leaders are born and not made. Some team members come to you fully formed as an A-Player, but most don't. My Jack in the Box experience taught me that more often than not, you have to do the work of turning newbies into A-Players. The work it takes is much more than being an inspirational leader; it's the blocking and tackling of proper hiring, training, direction, feedback, and recognition. But it's always worth the effort.

Consistently delivering a best-in-class customer experience starts with a shared understanding among a company's leaders that the quality of the customer experiences depends on the faces, hearts, and hands of your brand—namely, your customer-contact team members. The teammates at Corvirtus have been teaching this perspective for forty years or so and picture it as the *Corvirtus Egg Model*™. A simplified version of the model makes the relationship between the team member experience and the customer experience clear.

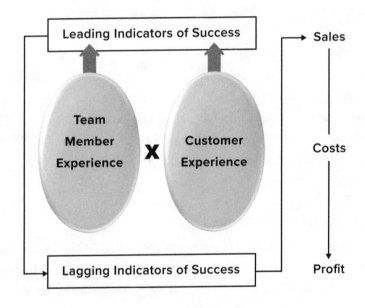

Corvirtus Egg Model

How do you change a customer's experience? When Lou Gerstner took over IBM in its darkest days, the company was hemorrhaging customers—and A-Players. The business model that had carried IBM to domination of its industry was now suffocating it, as more nimble and customer-centric competitors ate into IBM's customer and employee base. Gerstner saw at once that the problem was not the product or service (although each of them needed major revision), but instead the company's strong but unhealthy culture. It was a culture focused on pleasing management rather than wowing customers.

I remember attending a meeting of the senior leadership team. There must have been eighteen or so C-level executives in the room—and three times that number of their assistants. I guess their job was to assist. It was a practice that had prevailed for years, and worked for everyone except the customer. It had become a multilayered bureaucracy that isolated leadership from the customers and the team members who took care of them.

Gerstner cleaned house; executives who could not shift their focus from themselves to the customer were gone overnight. The company began asking customers what they wanted. In itself this was a major change from the past, when customers were told what they needed and what they needed happened to be what IBM was selling. What was different this time? Change. The change was a dance through the Egg Model and a recognition of how success happens.

I once taught a graduate course called "Complex Organizations." The message was that there is no such thing as a straight line in any organization. Everything that happens goes through something else that has to happen first and that has come through something else that had to happen before that, or the whole thing stops. Whew. Organizations are more like a circular firing squad than a straight line—rational, they are not.

The Egg Model represents the rippling effect of complexity and simplifies it in terms of what comes first. Fortunately, there is no question of what comes first in an organization: it's the employee experience, as there is no being customer-focused without first being employee-focused. I used the Egg way back then as a teaching tool.

First, I would lead a discussion of the multiplication sign. People know that any number multiplied by a zero is still a zero. You cannot have a great customer experience in the presence of a zippo employee experience; it won't happen—ever. I would make the point that A-Players and even B-Players will run from this situation. My intent was for the students to understand that *the team member experience is the upper limit to the quality of the customer experience.* So don't be stupid, get your team member experience right *first*, and your customer experience will follow.

Second, while this might seem counterintuitive, you cannot fix a poor customer experience by working on the customer experience itself. *The rule of thumb is that almost all improvement in the customer experience happens through the efforts of your team members, who are the faces, hearts, and hands of your customer experience.* In short, there are no knobs to turn on your customer experience, but there are lots of knobs to turn on your team member experience that can immediately improve your customer experience. The knobs are things like quality hiring procedures, training, clear direction, feedback, and recognition.

The model shows *leading indicators of success* for team members and customers as the direct results of the quality of their experiences. The leading indicators are *attitudinal* and typically expressed as *behavioral intentions*. Bad experiences equal bad intentions. For example, at the end of a shift, an hourly team member has one of three intentions:

1. "I can hardly wait to get back to work tomorrow: it was so great that I am going to name my cat after my team leader."

2. "It was okay; it pays the bills, and no one pissed me off today. I'll be there."

3. "If I'm lucky, I'll die during the night and will not have to work tomorrow."

It's often the little things about the team member's experience that determine intentions: Did you greet each team member as they came to work? Did you praise that team member for solving a customer's problem? Did you teach a team member a new skill? Did you say thank you when the team member finished his shift and was about to leave for home? Did you ask about a team member's sick child? These sorts of behaviors on your part create good intentions on the part of your team members. And these intentions mostly show up *as lagging indicators of success*. These are hard numbers, like team member turnover rate, proportion of managers promoted from within, and actual referrals to work. These actuals are the roots of the active loyalty of your customers and result in growth in sales and profit. It's that clear, and it's that simple.

Unscrambling the Team Member Egg

Corvirtus has surveyed hundreds of thousands of hourly and management employees over the long life of the company. The surveys typically measure team member perceptions of the quality of their experience, consequent intentions, and, sometimes, results. When we have done the additional work of linking team member intentions to outcomes, like employee turnover, sales per customer, and star ratings on social media, we have *never* failed to find a relationship. Good intentions lead to good things and bad intentions lead to bad things. It's that clear. So shaping your team members' perceptions of your leadership by providing a quality experience matters not only to you, but also to your customers and your bottom line.

Digging around in our survey database has also revealed that there is such a thing as a generic employee experience. This conclusion has been reinforced by our work with dozens of leadership teams as they strive to clarify and articulate their intended customer and employee experiences. It turns out that remarkable places to work are pretty much the same, regardless of the industry. I think about it in terms of team members wanting good answers from their leaders to five questions:

1. Where are we going?

2. What will it be like when we get there?

3. How will we get there?

4. Can you get us there?

5. What's in it for me if I make the journey with you?

When I show these questions to a leadership team, I'm inevitably asked, "So how do we answer their questions?" My answer for the last several years has revolved around keeping four promises that are at the heart of all employee experiences:

- **Clear Direction:** Ensuring that you understand our company's vision in detail; knowing where we are going and how your job contributes to getting us there; knowing what we stand for, as well as what we will not tolerate; communicating with you in a timely and clear manner in order to support your success; and keeping you up to speed on our priorities and any change that affects your ability to perform. *It is your being able to say, "I understand where we are going and my role in getting us there, our priorities, and what we stand for."*

- **Preparation:** Preparing you to achieve the results that are expected of you; adding to your knowledge and skills and providing the opportunity to practice them before being held accountable; and preparing you for the challenges not only of today, but tomorrow as well. *It is your being able to say, "I am ready to do my job to the standards expected of me and prepared for the opportunities of tomorrow."*

- **Support:** Clear, timely, honest, and actionable feedback on your behavior and results; challenging you to be better by identifying your strengths and opening your eyes to your opportunities; supporting your growth through guided learning opportunities; having the best team members to work with and the resources you need in order to succeed. *It is your being able to say, "I know what my opportunities are for growth and have the support I need to turn them into strengths."*

- **You Count:** Immediately welcoming you as a member of the team and helping you to feel included, valued, and respected; getting to know you and holding you accountable for your behavior and results; recognizing your contributions in ways that you value; and including you in the celebration of the team's success. *It is your being able to say, "I belong here, and I make a difference."*

I have used these generics countless times with different leadership teams for over thirty-five years as they work to articulate their intended employee experience. Inevitably, they are renamed, and details are added or subtracted depending on the team's beliefs and preferences, but no team has ever changed their essence. Sometimes, a team will add a promise or two. One of the favorite add-ons is a promise that focuses on being a fun place to work. That one makes sense to me.

The unchanging nature of the content of the promises over the years has taught me that there is a shared theme to all good places to work. After a team completes the content of their promises, I often convert them to a checklist, thereby creating a self-administered performance appraisal. To paraphrase Leo Tolstoy, "All good teams are good in the same way; each bad team finds its own way to be bad." The next chapter takes a look at the other side of the coin by diving into What Leaders Want.

LEADER TO-DO LIST

☐ List three opportunities for you to improve Clear Direction for your team.

☐ List three opportunities for you to improve Preparation for your team.

☐ List three opportunities for you to improve Support for your team.

☐ List three opportunities for you to improve You Count for your team.

☐ For each of the promises, pick the highest payoff opportunity and create an action plan that includes what you would expect to change within the team as a result of executing your plan.

7

MORE TO DO

SET CLEAR EXPECTATIONS

Team members should have all the freedom
they can handle, but only after they know the rules.

Sometimes people join your team fully formed as A-Players, but you can't count on it. Even then, it doesn't mean that they have the necessary skills to immediately hit it out of the park. Instead, what they have is an attitude that you can work with—one that says, "I am here to learn and contribute." Casey Hinson is definitely one of these. If you looked up A-Player attitude in the dictionary, you'd likely see a picture of Casey (and she definitely would be smiling).

Casey is the director of training for Metro Diner, Inc. She is smart, connecting, and inventive, and has made a huge contribution to the success of the company. Casey, Carl Sahlsten (her boss and the CEO of the company), and I teach a class once a month to newly promoted managers. The objective of the workshop is to introduce the newbies to the company's vision and culture. Casey is a big part of the success of the workshop. She contributed mightily to the design of the workshop and continues to be a big reason that it's so well received by the newly promoted managers. Carl and I are really good teachers; I'd say that Carl is close to Casey in his skill and ability to motivate the newbies. But Casey is in a class of her own: credible, knowledgeable, standard-setting, funny, enthusiastic, and totally organized. These are the "symptoms" of Casey's A-Playerness. The roots are in her total commitment to excellence, but I'll let Carl tell that story:[1]

> My partner told me about a new manager, Casey. She had worked for him at another restaurant company as a server and head wait (a lead person for a shift) while in college. I met Casey soon after at the pre-opening of a new location, where she was a brand-new assistant manager. When I walked into the restaurant, Casey was standing on a table conducting a training session for eighty new employees.
>
> I was immediately impressed with her poise and her command of the material she was teaching. Over the next nine months, she demonstrated leadership abilities beyond her time in management. She was "green" but smart, eager to learn, and willing to put in the work. She went out of her way to ask questions and shadow the general manager to learn new skills. As a result of her high performance, she was given the opportunity to open a new location as its general manager. That was less than a year after starting as an assistant manager. New openings are tough, but she was prepared and clearly determined to be successful by giving it 100 percent of her effort.
>
> As a brand-new GM, she initially struggled to achieve the necessary balance between taking care of her team members and customers on the one hand, and delivering the budgeted financial results on the other. But after some additional mentoring, she quickly mastered these skills. Casey learns very

quickly. She was great with her customers and built personal relationships by really getting to know them, their families, and their friends. From the get-go, she was always looking for new ways to drive her business forward, whether through catering, trying new promotions, or testing new specials. She was the GM of the restaurant for five years, during which she built it into a very successful business.

A couple of years later, my business partners and I partnered with the Davoli family. John Sr., John Jr., and Mark are the founders of Metro Diner in Jacksonville, Florida. They had four diners at the time, and together, we were looking to grow the brand at an accelerated pace. We knew the most important component of successfully growing the company was to have a strong culture and an equally strong training program.

Casey was the first person I thought of, and I invited her to join us as the director of training. It was an easy decision. From our very first interaction, it was clear how passionate, creative, and energetic she is. She's a natural teacher and conducted herself with more maturity and leadership than her years would indicate. She is smart, hardworking, dedicated, compassionate, and fun. Casey is also a constant advocate of Quality, never accepting "good enough" on the plate or at the table. And her smile and fun-loving approach definitely make Metro Diner a fun place to work.

She created almost all of our training systems and materials from scratch, mastered our POS system, and rolled out our online training for both hourly team members and managers. Casey embraces new ideas and technology with enthusiasm— all she cares about is whether they make a difference. Over the years, we have thrown countless projects her way. She catches them on the fly and takes them on as if they were her own ideas.

Casey has helped shape and develop our culture in so many ways. She played a big part working with the founders, my partners and me, and the folks at Corvirtus to put the culture of Metro Diner down on paper and make it teachable. She is the first impression of Metro Diner—and a great one—for so many new managers and team members. I have received many, many calls and emails from new joint venture partners and managers telling me how impressed they are with her and how excited it made them feel about joining Metro Diner.

I've also heard many times that our training materials and systems are more advanced than those of other organizations at the same stage in their development. Having witnessed her doing openings, speaking at leadership meetings, putting together manager in training meetings, doing follow-up MIT visits at diners, and so many more situations, it is clear Casey is a champion of Metro Diner.

She sees what needs to be done and does it. For example, in response to so many new managers arriving at the Coffee Break (the meeting for newbies) unprepared, Casey took it upon herself to produce a ten-minute video that set expectations for the attendees. Overnight, it literally changed the quality of the participation and speed of the MITs learning our vision and culture. She has been instrumental in growing the Metro Diner brand and has contributed to our success in a significant way.

Casey is definitely an A-Player, probably an A+ Player. But how do you make sense of her contribution? I know both Carl and Casey very well. There is no question that Carl sets clear direction; however, Casey's contribution is largely a reflection of who she is as a person. She is very much like many of my teammates at Corvirtus—prepared, motivated, and smart.

A-Players are great to have when you can find them, but there are not enough out there to ensure your team's success; hence, you have to "mold" A-Players through an effective recruiting and hiring system coupled with equally effective training procedures and the most important input of all: your leadership. Most new hires are C-Players, with some B-Players and a couple of A-Players here and there. The challenge is getting your new B- and C-Players to step up to being A-Players.

THEN, OF COURSE, THERE'S REALITY

If you think about the wish list for a team member, you can see the Caseys of the world all over it: *someone who shows up on time and is ready to work, works hard and well, looks for ways to contribute, supports other team members, speaks well of the company and its leaders, recommends the company to other good people as a place to work or do business, stays, and grows.* Casey is among those team members who make a leader's life easy, so you have to wonder why A-Players are so rare. I think a big part of the explanation is that there are so few A-Leaders—that is, Adored Leaders.

For one thing, excellence is, by definition, rare—or is it? Perhaps we don't know it when we see it, as there is overwhelming evidence that most people (including leaders) are not that good at judging the potential of job candidates. In fact, the data show that the people picking the skills of most leaders do so on the same level as flipping a coin. They are as prone to the same mistakes and stereotypes as anyone else.

Norman Brinker was an example. He founded Steak & Ale Restaurants and was one of the early leaders of Jack in the Box. Norman was a charismatic and creative entrepreneur who essentially invented the casual dining segment of the restaurant industry. He also, rightly, had a reputation for incubating some of the best restaurant leaders in the industry. It is fair to say that Norman had a good feel for leaders. One day, in a conversation about leadership, I asked him how he identifies potential. One of the tricks he described to me was, "I look to see how they sit in the chair when I am talking to them." Curious, I asked what that told him, and he answered, "If they sit forward, it tells me how much energy they have."

It's hard to argue with success, but I consulted with the company for several years, and Norman picked many more duds than A-Players; it's just that no one remembers the duds. But then again, picking people was not the key to his success, but rather something else altogether: Norman had that rare mixture of creativity, aggression, charisma, and, most important, the patience to allow people to stretch themselves, to safely fail, and, from that experience, to grow. That latter quality saved many of the leaders who worked for him and who later went on to found their own companies or to successfully lead other restaurant companies.

But I think there is something else that explains the shortage of A-Players. In an earlier chapter, I noted that my company has surveyed hundreds of thousands of managers, individual contributors, and hourly employees over the years. If there is one common complaint that cuts across all employee levels, it is a lack of *Clear Direction*. Employees would cite the lack of an inspiring vision or purpose, hazy and jumpy priorities, and ambiguous expectations of them. Something else that was often cited is the absence of the element of *You Count*, and it was not what you might expect. It was *the failure to hold people accountable*.

My conclusion from the consistency of these findings is not flattering to the leadership profession: B- and C-leaders don't attract or retain A-Players. Once a leader puts someone on the team, what the team member needs is the same thing that all team members need: *Clear Direction, Preparation, Support,* and *You Count.* These are the four promises kept by Adored Leaders. Employees also want to know the rules of success—that is, what the leader expects of them. That's part of Clear Direction.

What Do You Want from Me?

It is not surprising that "What do you want from me?" is a question at the heart of all relationships, human and otherwise. For example, my dog Sochi never quits asking that question. She has this dogged need to know the rules, and if not told she makes them up on the fly, and never do her made-up rules favor peace and quiet. It turns out that dogs and people share an aversion to chaos. We both strongly prefer relationships that are predictable, and, in the absence of clear rules, we will make them up in pretty much the same way that Sochi does—that is, to favor ourselves.

While it's our nature to love surprises of kindness—a compliment, encouragement—we revolt at a surprise change in expectations and direction, as in, "So why didn't you tell me that's what you wanted in the first place?" Stress, not excitement, is the natural reaction to chaos. People simply need to know the rules and, knowing them, how to follow them. Clarity saves time, stress, conflict, and disappointment—yours and your team members'. If what you want someone to contribute to a relationship is not what they want to give to it, they will move on to another relationship where the exchange works. It's called employee turnover. If they can't move on, they will change the rules, if they can, by producing less, being less compliant with your direction, and bringing the spirit of your team down.

Just like it is for Sochi, the rules and actions your team members create in the absence of direction will have the effect of minimizing the maximum disruption you can inflict on them. This is how relationships work, within and outside of the workplace. When you fail to set expectations and provide clear direction, people will fill the vacuum created by chaos and, thereby, shift the leadership of the team from the leader to the team members—and not always in ways that support the success of the team.

A-PLAYERS ARE BORN—AND MADE

Casey was born with what it takes to be an A-Player—sort of—but she has also been parented and has had mentors who maximized her ability to enthusiastically commit to a team, take responsibility for herself, and perform at a high level. That's true of most of the teammates in my own company: many were A-Players from the get-go, but a much larger number grew into that kind of contribution by having worked for the Adored Leaders who have been part of our team over the years.

It's natural for a leader to blame mediocre performance on the team member, and it's unnatural for a leader to blame it on themselves. But leadership is unquestionably part of the problem. I'd go so far as to say this: *setting clear performance expectations is the biggest opportunity for many leaders to substantially improve their team's performance.* Setting clear expectations was what Coach Wooden was doing with his "how to put on your socks and tie your shoes" lesson. He was telling his team members not to lose merely because they failed to control something they had total control over.

Three Expectations

Over the years I have met many, many A-Players and had the pleasure of working with a whole bunch of them. I have also had long conversations with leaders about what makes a team member an A-Player. When you read the story of Casey Hinson's contribution to her team, it's almost overwhelming in its breadth and depth. The challenge is to look at the many things that she does well and use them to set clearer direction for your team members. Is there a pattern to what high performers do that you can use to set expectations for your team members? The answer is "Yes."

Over the years of working with leadership teams and with our own team to understand performance, three themes have emerged in terms of What Leaders Want: *Citizenship, Teamwork,* and *Getting After It.* These are *the categories of leader expectations of team members.*

Citizenship: Accepting responsibility for yourself and the success of your team; arriving on time, ready to work and being responsible for your words and actions; following all policies, performing to standard, and never ignoring something that needs to be done; making decisions based on our beliefs and values; asking for help before it is too late and never playing the blame game; enthusiastically supporting a decision once it has been made; protecting the property of the company and your team; and treating others with respect, understanding, caring, and fairness.

Teamwork: Knowing your job and how it meshes with jobs of your team; jumping in to help without being asked; challenging other team members when their behavior detracts from the team's mission; being open to challenging your behavior and results; and stepping forward to recommend changes that you believe will help the team to improve.

Getting After It: Lifting the spirit of others by being positive, eager to serve, and enthusiastic about your team; using your head before you use your hands; looking on the bright side; being fun to be around; moving with a sense of urgency; and celebrating the success of your team and its members.

Is there anything missing from these three promises from team members that you would add? I doubt it. These are the promises from team members to their team and to the company. They're a rich resource that you can use for setting clear expectations of individual team members. As an example, after editing these promises to suit your particular team, you could use them in a new team member orientation to set expectations. One of the things that works particularly well is to convert the definition into a checklist like the following example:

Citizenship: Being a contributing team member by . . .

- Accepting responsibility for yourself and the success of the team
- Arriving on time and ready to work
- Being responsible for your words and actions
- Following all policies and procedures
- Performing to the standards of your job
- Never ignoring something that needs to be done
- Making decisions based on our beliefs and values
- Asking for help before it is too late
- Never playing the blame game
- Enthusiastically supporting a decision once it has been made
- Protecting the property of the company, our customers, and other team members
- Treating everyone with respect, understanding, caring, and fairness

This is a format that works well with new hires to set performance expectations. I have found it's best to use examples of specific behavior (e.g., "Open the door for the customer") to illustrate each element of the checklist.

You could also use this checklist to get a handle on the performance of one of your team members in much the same way you evaluated your own behavior in the last chapter, by asking yourself, "Does this team member typically do what is described in this promise?" Give it a "Yes" or "No" answer. For every "Yes" answer, write down a specific example of the team member's behavior that you have personally seen. For every "No" answer, write down a specific example that you would like to see.

By the way, if you cannot recall specific examples that you have seen (rather than heard about), you should consider whether you are the one who should be evaluating the team member or whether you should pay closer attention to the team member's behavior. You can also further embed the promises in your team's culture by teaching and reinforcing them through daily coaching, team meetings, regular performance conversations, and evaluating candidates for promotion.

Regardless of your business or industry, the clarity and quality of your expectations will either accelerate or hinder your journey to being an Adored Leader. It's like Charles F. Kettering (American inventor, engineer, and businessman) said: "The level of our expectations determines the level of our action. High achievement always takes place in the framework of high expectations." That is so true, and to add to his insight: *the source of the high expectations does not matter nearly as much as their clarity.* High-performance teams very often set high-performance standards for themselves once they have melded as a team. Regardless of who sets them, you might be surprised at how the introduction of high standards can affect performance—and in a spirited way.

LEADER TO-DO LIST

☐ What are the expectations you have for your team that cut across all team members?

☐ What have you done to ensure that these expectations are understood?

☐ Think about each member of your team individually and write down the expectations you have of that team member.

☐ Communicate your expectations to the team as a whole and to each individual team member.

8

MEASURE

MAKING A DIFFERENCE

Of course, the numbers can lie,
but not the right ones.

I've never been keen on accountability—especially when it's me who is being held accountable. Being reminded that I've not held up my end of the bargain in a relationship is stressful and embarrassing. Fortunately, there is a positive side to the coin of accountability, as it also means that "You count" and "We need you." In this light, accountability is simply another example of creating a sense of belonging and significance. It's a signal to your team members that their contribution matters—that they are significant to the team.

Most of us like the belonging and significance part of "You Count" a lot. But if you're going to lead, you have to get over the "uphold your commitments" part of accountability and instead focus on accountability's importance to the growth of your team and you. Accountability fuels a team toward high performance and, more often than not, to achieving superior results.

Adding good measurement to the mix is a great way to leverage accountability into a tool for personal and team growth. While I've seen instances in which what gets measured isn't treasured, mostly it is. That's particularly true when the metrics are linked to things people care about, such as compensation, promotion, and recognition. The fact that what gets measured gets treasured tells you that deciding what to measure and how to measure it are among the more important decisions you will make.

THE FACES, HEARTS, AND HANDS OF YOUR BRAND

In most service industries—restaurants, health care, airlines, banking, and hotels—employee turnover can kill a company's dream of leaving its best competitors behind. I have worked with companies in each of these industries and continue to be surprised that their leaders pay so little attention to building employee retention. It defies reason to think that you can have regular customers without having regular employees to recognize them. To make my point: think of how many times you have been asked by a restaurant server "Is this your first visit?" when you have been there several times. Just the other day, I was in the bank where we have banked for more than twenty years only to be asked for my identification, as there were no tellers working that day who recognized me.

Throughout the many years of my career, lots of progress has been made in understanding employee retention and its causes. However, little progress has been made with respect to accurately measuring retention, its value, or in developing ways to manage it. For example, anyone who has ever been a customer knows that it feels special to be recognized (it's that belonging thing again), and anyone who has ever led a team knows the value of A-Players.

But awareness of the contribution of these competent, confident, and proud faces to building a customer base seems not to have sunk in enough among leaders to cause concerted action to build employee retention. There are lots of explanations for this intentional ignorance, but the one that makes the most sense turns out to be a really poor excuse: *habit*. In this case, it is the habit of not measuring it or its consequences.

High employee turnover has historically been accepted as a cost of doing business that must be endured in the industries characterized by service employees, especially entry-level employees. That certainly was the message I got when I opened my first Jack in the Box. The upshot of it was that I should try to stay ahead of employee turnover by constantly interviewing job applicants. In effect, the best advice was to get used to something that is largely unmanageable, a cost of doing business that appeared nowhere on my P&L. Nonetheless, it dramatically affected my business and bottom line. Lesson learned: *what does not get measured does not get treasured.*

The Restaurant Industry, for Example

While I'm dissing the restaurant industry, I may as well dig in a bit more. The hourly turnover rate in the industry is far north of 100 percent at the time of this writing, due to a full-employment economy. What this means is that *the typical restaurant's entire staff is replaced more than once each year.* So much for the value of familiar faces. Judging simply by the numbers, you might be inclined to conclude that high employee turnover is a characteristic of the restaurant industry, except that it's not: *it's a characteristic of individual restaurants!*

When employee turnover is measured as one employee discontinuing employment at a restaurant, the more-than-100 percent number makes sense. However, if you look at the number from a leadership perspective, the number grossly understates the "stickiness" or retention of employees within the industry itself. By that, I mean employees (management and hourly) tend to quit one restaurant only to immediately go to work for another restaurant. Thus while they leave a single restaurant in large numbers, they leave the industry in relatively small numbers. Proof of this assertion is that the turnover-out-of-the-industry is closer to 20 percent than the 100 percent commonly cited. In fact, this number is comparable to many other industries, which leads me to an important conclusion: *employees quit their leaders, not the place or industry that employs them.*

Why would they leave the restaurant industry? It's the single largest path to a six-figure income for people without a college education! Like a lot of service industries, it's a first job, but for hundreds of thousands of management and hourly employees, it becomes a career. In a nutshell, the industry is a reasonably stable employment platform characterized by lots of employee *churn*, or movement from one restaurant employer to another. It amounts to an industry-wide game of musical chairs played in response to appointed and accepted leaders and a lack of Adored Leaders.

If you are a leader in the restaurant industry, or any industry for that matter, you should be totally miffed that people quit you to work for someone else in the same industry. It has always miffed me when a teammate (what Corvirtus calls employees) quits for that reason. In fact, it's not only miff-making, but it hurts my feelings as well. I think the right perspective to have on turnover is this: *a high turnover rate is a comment on the quality of your leadership in terms of the four promises to team members.*

This perspective is particularly true when team members quit to take an essentially identical job elsewhere. It's what you'd expect from an accepted leader, but not from an Adored Leader. While team members quitting is a serious leadership problem, its solution starts with understanding its sources—which is partly a measurement problem.

CRACKING THE TEAM MEMBER EGG

I am going to "crack" the Team Member Egg from the Corvirtus Egg Model first presented in chapter 6 to illustrate the measurement knowledge and actions necessary to make the leap from accepted to Adored Leader. The Egg Model is a marvelously useful tool (if I do say so myself) for understanding team member behavior and teaching leaders how to manage it.

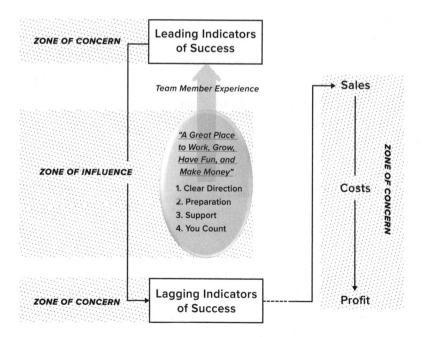

The Corvirtus Egg Model

I've been dying to use a certain in-fashion word for the past seven chapters, and, finally, my opportunity has arrived. That word is "deconstruct," and we are going to *deconstruct* the Team Member Egg in order to help you to answer a very important question: "How good a leader am I?" Deconstructing that puppy will also help you to zero in on the "knobs to turn" in order to ramp-up your leadership skills. The deconstruction will start with the yolk—*team member experience*—and go from there.

The Team Member Experience

I remember learning about the five senses—*sight, taste, touch, smell,* and *hearing*—in grade school. The idea that I could be aware that something was happening before I understood what was happening intrigued me. I, of course, had never thought of it until Miss Vance, my teacher, used a now familiar example to illustrate how it works. When you put your hand on a hot stove, your sense of touch tells you that something is wrong before your brain brings you up to speed about what exactly is wrong and what to do about it. That's when your brain yells, "You are burning! Move your hand!"

The same kind of thing happens with your team members: they hear what you say and see what you do and, *bam*, conclude whether it's good or bad. Sometimes they back into a conclusion: Does what you say and do support their success, or is it something that takes away from it? The best-case scenario is that it's something that fits into being *a great place to work, grow, have fun, and make money.* If so, they have experienced your words and actions as *Clear Direction, Preparation, Support,* and *You Count* in ways that strengthen their sense of belonging and significance and feelings of competence, confidence, and pride.

Simply put, your team members hear what you say and see what you do and then categorize their experience of you into one of two buckets: Good Stuff or Bad Stuff. For example, you hold a team meeting to explain an important change in direction for the team. You think you are setting Clear Direction, and they hear you. But which bucket are they putting your words and actions into?

Is it the good or the bad bucket? Which one they choose not only has to do with what you just said and did, but also whether you've earned their trust. In most team members' minds it's not a "sort of" thing, but a definite yes or no: your words and actions have either been projecting integrity, credibility, and balance or they haven't, and based on what they experience, they chose the appropriate bucket.

These kinds of mental gyrations on the part of team members serve to reinforce the need for you to be predictable and consistent. In the example, you are trying to keep the promises of Clear Direction and Support, but it's your team members who decide whether you are moving the needle on being adored, or not. They do it by comparing what you said to their prior experience of you—to your habits of character in each moment of their experience.

If your behavior has been unpredictable and misunderstood in the past, it will be discounted and likely put into the bad bucket. This is an area where working through some of your own examples is most helpful, but I'll provide a small taste here, using the definition of Clear Direction introduced in chapter 6.

- **Clear Direction:** Ensuring that you understand our company's vision in detail; knowing where we are going and how your job contributes to getting us there; knowing what we stand for, as well as what we will not tolerate; communicating with you in a timely and clear manner in order to support your success; and keeping you up to speed on our priorities and any change that affects your ability to perform. *It is you being able to say, "I understand where we are going and my role in getting us there, our priorities, and what we stand for."*

This is what Clear Direction looks like as a complete thought, but you can also look at it as a list of behaviors. An abbreviated list for Clear Direction looks like the following one:

Clear **Direction** is *me* ensuring that each team member . . .

☐ Understands the vision of the team in detail

☐ Knows how their job contributes to the team's success

☐ Is clear on what I will stand for, as well as what I will not stand for

☐ Is communicated with in a timely and clear manner about anything that affects their success

☐ Knows the team's priorities

Put a checkmark in the box if it's true and leave it blank if it is not. (*There are no "mostly true" checks, only true or false.*) For every box that you have checked as being true about your words and actions, write a two-sentence example of your behavior that validates your self-assessment of that element of Clear Direction. For the ones that you have not checked, write a two-sentence commitment to what you will do in order to make it true of your words and actions. In this way, you can self-measure your performance and compare it to your team's evaluation of your leadership via, for example, an annual Team Member Experience Survey.

All this talk about words and actions reminds me of something that I often caution leaders about. As a leader, you don't get to think out loud, as everything you say is taken as gospel by one or more of your team members. You are no longer just speaking among friends, even though your team members may be friends of yours.

Being in charge carries with it the special burden of discretion, and discretion is the first part of integrity. If you don't want to have your integrity questioned, consider your thoughts before sharing them. I recommend sleeping on it for at least twenty-four hours before saying anything that affects the performance of your team. Do that, and what you will discover is that some things that seemed critical were only important and can wait or be kept silent.

Inconsistent and unpredictable leaders deliver an inconsistent and unpredictable team member experience. As a result, they cannot count on receiving the benefit of the doubt from their team members when it comes to the integrity or credibility of their efforts. This is why—regardless of your political views—President Trump has so much trouble having good intentions or wisdom associated with his decisions, even if they make sense. As far as I can tell, "Fire! Ready? Aim!" has never been a confidence-building leadership strategy. Nonetheless, it's the one most often used by accepted leaders. If what you say and do makes sense and you have made sense in the past, it will go into the good bucket; otherwise, no way.

FRETTING ABOUT THE RIGHT STUFF

The question is not whether you fret, as we all fret about this or that. The issue is whether you fret about the right stuff—that is, stuff you can actually do something about. But what is the right stuff to fret about among all the stuff we are faced with on a daily basis? Thankfully, most of it can easily be sorted into one of three categories:

1. I can't do anything about this stuff: it's totally out of my control.

2. I can fix this stuff: it's totally under my control.

3. I can help to fix this stuff: it's something I can influence, if I try.

The stuff in the first category is governed by external forces. It includes things like the state of the labor market, the weather, and the economy. The stuff in the second category is all about you, as it is made up of your decisions and behavior. Do you consistently keep your four promises to your team members? Does your customer experience create a sense of belonging and significance for your customers? Do you stretch yourself or stay in your comfort zone? This kind of stuff is totally under your control. Do your team members always respond positively when you consistently keep your four promises to them? Do your team members consistently keep their three promises to the team and to you? This kind of stuff is partly under your control and partly under each team member's control. However, you can definitely influence their response by hiring the right team members and holding them accountable and getting rid of the wrong team members before they corrupt the spirit of your team. Thinking about the stuff that you have to deal with on a daily basis and putting it into one of the three categories will go a long way toward relieving the stress inherent in leadership. Be concerned about the stuff in your Zones of Concern and then act to influence them through your decisions and behavior in your Zone of Influence.

Leading Indicators of Success

The flow in the egg is from the Team Member Experience up through the Team Member Goal, to affect Team Member Intentions and Satisfaction. Intention is not behavior; it's not even words spoken out loud. Rather, intentions are "want-to-dos" generated by the nature of the team member's experience, for example: Did it make the team *a great place to work* or *a great place to grow* or *a great place to have fun* or *a great place to make money?* If it's "Yes!" to any of these, then there is a high likelihood of positive intentions. Whether actual behavior is the result of these intentions depends on two things: the *intensity* of the feeling and the team member's *ability* to do something about it.

Here's an example of how this works: I have a pacemaker, so I have to go through a bunch of routine tests every five years. One day, I had an appointment with my cardiologist at 3:00 p.m. to initiate the process. This was the second time that I had seen him. I was on time; in fact I was early, even though the first time I met him he was thirty minutes late for our appointment. It's a good thing that I brought a good thick book to this appointment.

After fifteen minutes of waiting for the appointment, I was a bit agitated. Even a very good book could not hold my attention. At the half-hour mark, I was up and reading the notices on the wall and examining a life-size plastic heart on the countertop. At the forty-five-minute mark, I was totally pissed. I felt *disrespected* and *uncared* for; clearly, the doctor had completely blown two of the four cornerstones of a good relationship. That's when he walked into the examination room. No explanation. No apology. Just small talk. I was thinking to myself, "You arrogant bastard!" I was steaming (inside), and that little voice in my head that sometimes yells at me said, "Stand up and walk out of here!" But then the other little voice that I discovered only later in life rescued me from myself, saying, "Tom: Listen to me! You have to have these tests, you spent the time already, so get over yourself." This self-talk sort of thing is what all people do, including your team members in reaction to their experience of your leadership—good or bad. Think about it the next time you are late for a team meeting. Team members hear what you say, while your behavior shouts about what you really mean.

That little gray arrow in the Egg Model pointing from the Team Member Experience to Leading Indicators reflects the power of the Team Member Experience to create team member intentions. Essentially, these are behavioral *intentions* and are the first-level outcomes of an experience of your leadership. Intentions range from really bad to really good and include important stuff like intention to perform and stay; intention to commit, grow, and learn; intention to refer good people for employment; and intention to share the experience with the team member's friends on social media.

Let's take the intention to stay as an example. It's the end of Jane's workday. By her reckoning, it's been a day much like any other. This might sound like a description of a ho-hum workday, but that's not necessarily true. That depends on the quality of her day and how typical it is overall. Suppose it was a great workday, and just one of many great days. The first thing you might notice is that Jane just volunteered to stay over to get some necessary work done, even while other team members are leaving. Even though she leaves late, Jane goes home energized and can hardly wait to get back to work tomorrow. She is an actively loyal team member—enthusiastic and committed. The team is important to her, and she *feels* as though she is part of it—that she belongs and is significant.

Lagging Indicators of Success

Jane's intentions show up as behavior: such as volunteering to cover a shift, working hard, suggesting improvements, referring a new team member to you, smoothly handling a difficult customer, participating in team meetings, and showing interest in the management training program. In this sense, *lagging indicators of success are intentions or leading indicators brought to life.*

And while there is not perfect 100 percent symmetry between team member intentions and behavior, there is a strong relationship between the two; for example, every team member who goes home angry and thinking about quitting does not actually quit, but a fair number of them do, given the opportunity. Knowing your team members' intentions today gives you a leg up on what will happen in the future and the opportunity to head off a serious problem, such as the loss of A-Players.

The Zones of Concern

There are three *Zones of Concern* in the Team Member Egg: leading indicators, lagging indicators, and financial results. Within each Zone of Concern are things that you care about as they affect your team's stability and ability. Unfortunately, they are not things that you can impact directly (with few exceptions). With respect to the Team Member Egg, the content of the Zones of Concern include the following:

LEADING INDICATORS	LAGGING INDICATORS	FINANCIAL RESULTS
• Job Satisfaction	• Turnover Rate	• Real Sales Growth
• Intent to Perform	• Tenure	• Controllable Costs
• Intent to Refer	• Percentage of Hires from Referral	• Cash Flow
• Intent to Stay	• Bench Strength	• Real Profit Growth

There is not a single outcome within any of the Zones of Concern that is not a big deal. You might like to add others suitable to your situation, like team member productivity or social media ratings. The only caveat is that you should be able to accurately measure it. The downside of lagging indicators and financial results is that they are measures of history; that is, they have already occurred, and you can do nothing about them—sort of.

The "sort of" means that by measuring intentions—leading indicators—you can act on them *before* they become permanent behaviors and choices. A lot depends on the frequency and quality of your measurement. If you are measuring the intent to quit on an annual basis or even on a quarterly basis, you'll not be able to influence them nearly as much as if you measure them on a daily basis. This sounds impossible, but it isn't. All you need to have is a shift or workday assessment (at Corvirtus, we call these Pulse Surveys) that measures the few critical determinants of employee perceptions of a shift very well. This measure would be administered at the end of a shift and would ask questions like, "Based on the quality of today's shift, how likely are you to quit your job in the next month or so?" You can even use a bit of humor, such as, "Based on the quality of your shift today, how likely is it that you will sing songs about [the company]?" If you wanted to be a little less obvious about the purpose of your measure, you might ask, "Based on the quality of your workday, how likely are you to recommend to your friends that they apply for a job at [name of company]?" The assumption here is that people do not recommend places to their friends that they themselves do not like.

By using a Pulse Survey or your own method, you can know definitively what's linked to intentions to stay, leave, and perform. This allows you to take swift and confident action instead of looking through a mountain of data. Good measurement gives you the power of knowing that, let's say, incomplete training and support for new team members are driving their intentions to leave.

You can act on the lagging indicators by taking specific actions on the leading indicators—with great intention and accuracy because of your measurement. For example, you can decrease short-term employee turnover (churn) by doing what some employers do: pay a "tenure bonus." However, if that becomes a long-term strategy, all you are doing is raising the effective wage rate to where it should have been in order to compete for labor, *given the quality of your current team member experience.* The same goes for referral bonuses. These various metrics do one thing: help you to focus on the highest payoff fixes for the real problems. Those real problems will always show up as part of the four promises to team members.

As you might have guessed, I'm not a fan of short-term brain-less fixes, like signing bonuses or tenure bonuses. Tactics like these amount to nothing more than a short-term manipulation in that they are not related to the quality of the team member experience. They may even be cunning short-term solutions, but they are not leadership in the sense that it was defined in chapter 1, in terms of "earned" loyalty and "molding [team members] into a high-performance team." The long and short of it is that each of the Zones of Concern shown in the Egg Model contain important outcomes that you very much care about, but they are ones that you manage only by directing your attention to the *Zone of Influence.*

Zone of Influence

I've already given the secret away. Solutions are in the Zone of Influence. It's the Team Member Experience where you focus your effort to change the outcomes in the three Zones of Concern. What this means is simple: to get what you want (e.g., good intentions, low turnover, and sales growth), you do what team members want (i.e., Clear Direction, Preparation, Support, and You Count). *The knobs to turn on earning the active loyalty of your team members and molding them into a high-performance team are on the four promises to team members.* What I like about this fact of team life is that it serves to focus your attention on the things over which you have 100 percent control: namely, your words and actions.

That's what the simple example using Clear Direction earlier in this chapter demonstrates. When you combine your candidly honest and painful self-assessment with what your team members tell you in a Team Member Experience Report (TMER), you are able to converge on what matters to them and what needs to be changed in order to earn their active loyalty. In this regard, a People Profit and Loss Statement is a useful tool for tracking your Team Member Experience.

As a rule of thumb, if something is a negative in your TMER, it's *probably* a negative in fact, and you should take the steps necessary to turn it into a positive. If it's a negative in your self-assessment of your performance via the four promises to team members *and* it's in the TMER, it is definitely a negative, and you'd be foolish not to jump on it. What you don't want to do is what a lot of leaders do: deny the validity of your team members' feedback. That's a recipe for staying an accepted leader or, quite possibly, slipping back into being an appointed leader.

FINAL THOUGHTS

An Adored Leader earns the active loyalty of team members and molds them into a high-performance team. Given the wisdom of "what gets measured gets treasured," a leader's future very much depends upon the quality and clarity of thinking applied to defining success and identifying how it is achieved. The gold standard for metrics is that they tap directly into this thinking. *While you don't typically stop to think about it, it's the clarity of these thoughts that gets measured and become treasured.* Bad thinking equals bad measurement equals bad results. Bad thinking—like the cry to "exceed expectations"—is but one example, as it assumes that everyone has the same expectations, that you know what they are, and that you can address them one at a time. This is a lot of wasted thinking and energy.

Hopefully, this introduction to how measurement can support you on your path to being an Adored Leader has prepared you to participate in the development and use of good metrics. What's most important is that you have a rational approach to the creation and use of good measurement in the service of your team. In a world of "faster is better" and "new is old," good measurement is an indispensable tool to getting things right and, by doing so, making progress toward being an Adored Leader.

LEADER TO-DO LIST

☐ List the measures that you currently use in order to gauge the quality of the team member experience you are delivering.

☐ In terms of the Team Member Egg, what are the gaps in what you are currently measuring?

☐ Create a plan for filling the gaps in your team member metrics.

9

BEING STICKY

NOT SO FAST!

Failing is the painful part of learning
how to succeed.

eadership takes place in a rocking boat, whether your boat is company, nonprofit, or some other form of enterprise. Things are always changing. Sometimes it's so quick that it catches you off guard. At other times it evolves so slowly that it sneaks up on you. In either case, it's a surprise. This constant motion is one of the things that makes the study of leadership so interesting, and hard.

I published a book in 2008 that took me more than thirty years to write.[1] It's not that I'm a slow writer or even a slow learner. I think a better explanation is that some things take a long time and a lot of experience to understand, and that includes understanding what's true, what you're good at, and how to combine the two. It took me all of those years to learn what I needed to learn, discover some of the myths of enterprise-building, and the things that I thought I was good at but was not. It also took time for me to develop a voice clear enough to share what I've learned, be open to criticism for sharing it, and the courage to stay on course.

The reviews of that first book were consistently very positive—five stars on Amazon. That was a whoop-whoop for me; however, it didn't translate to sales. I was hoping for the best-seller list, but the book sold only a bit more than 4,500 copies. I try to see the bright side of things, so that's a success in my book (no pun intended), because the people who read it found it to be useful. Which brings me around to my point: *the drive to be useful is a hallmark of the Adored Leader.*

In contrast, this book took about three months to write the first draft. One reason for the shorter time frame is that I have more time to write than I used to. More likely, as I thought about it, the real reason for the shorter time is that this book is an extension of the first one. The subtitle of the first book was *How to Build a Company Reputation for Human Goodness, Flawless Execution, and Being Best-In-Class.* In retrospect, the subtitle could've been *How to Earn the Active Loyalty of All of Your Stakeholders.* The books are alike in that the difference-maker for leaders and enterprise builders is character and achievement.

The two books are different sides of the same coin—namely, *excellence.* The first book took up the side of macro-level excellence in that it applies to developing character and achievement at the enterprise level. This one takes up the side of micro-level excellence in that it applies to developing character and achievement at the individual level. That's you, rather than where you apply your skills—the enterprise. What I have realized is that the principles of what it takes to be an Adored Leader are not all that different from what it takes to be an Adored Company—one that I describe in the first book as having "glow." So it is that Adored Leaders also have a "glow" to them.

THE JOURNEY NEVER ENDS

Let's do a bit of a review. While we work backward in the book, it's important to remember that measurement tells you whether you are passing the *ultimate test of leadership; namely, the presence of followers*. Then there is chapter 7's guidance on setting clear expectations (the weakest skill of most every leader I have ever known). But before you can set clear expectations, chapter 6 identifies the promises to team members that you have to keep—this is fertile ground for setting expectations. Chapter 5 is one of my favorites, as it dives into the tangible advantage of being a well-mannered leader, making the point that there is always a market for kindness—especially among your A-Players. Its message is clear and simple: there is no room for jerks in the world of leadership.

Chapter 4 defines the five cornerstones of any positive relationship—respect, understanding, caring, fairness, and fun—and is therefore foundational to being an Adored Leader, dad, mom, or friend. Chapter 3 stresses the importance of creating positive mindsets in your team members and explains why those mindsets are universally craved by team members. When the going gets tough for a team, its mindset or sense of confidence and pride in itself is often the difference between winning and losing. In a nutshell, *Adored Leaders have a knack for making team members feel successful.* Chapter 2 touches on the overriding importance of the sense of belonging and significance not only in the life of a team, but also in life in general. It's a piece of understanding that you can take to the bank whether you are dealing with your team members, children, friends, neighbors—it's about being constructive and valued. I would like you to think about these first eight chapters as providing a strong foundation for building your Leadership Edge. The only thing left to do is to put it into action—a little bit at a time. And as you do, keep in mind that failure is an important part of growth.

If you've made good use of the suggestions sprinkled throughout the prior eight chapters, you likely consider yourself ready to begin your journey to being an Adored Leader. Good for you, but here's a red flag alert: there's a world of difference between the "Ready? Aim! Fire!" approach I recommend and the "Fire! Ready? Aim!" approach of many leaders. I can tell you from personal experience that it's not a good way to lead.

I Hear Your Words, but It's Your Behavior That Shouts at Me

I've never met an accepted leader who was not intelligent or, at least, intelligent enough. However, I've known lots of them who were not all that wise or savvy. By that I mean that they were not able to get the most out of what their DNA and life experience had given them to work with. One clue was their tendency to repeatedly do the same thing, somehow hoping for a different outcome. Another was their habit of copying what other leaders were doing in the blind hope that it would work for them too.

That's not what Adored Leaders do. Many of the ones I have known were very intelligent in a horsepower sense, but most of them were not in that category. However, all of them were very smart—that is, wise in the ways of getting things done. Building rockets is rocket science; leadership is not. It's more a process of paying attention and learning from your experiences, putting that learning to work for the betterment of your team, and being predictable. Wisdom is available to everyone, as it's something you acquire by being open and ready to learn, stepping out of your comfort zone, and embracing the risk of personal failure. The ultracompetitive nature of many leaders makes this last—and crucial—characteristic the hardest to adopt.

A significant part of leadership is being prepared for opportunity when it comes along. In this light, your competition isn't other leaders—you have little control over them—it's you, and being well prepared to succeed! It's you beginning with the end in mind of earning the active loyalty of your team members.

Why? For the simple reason that you are not the one who does the work of winning; your team does the heavy lifting. When you work on creating a sense of confidence, competence, and pride in your team members, you are by definition creating winners for today and the future. And when you do that, everything else seems to magically fall into place.

It's much more than leading people and understanding the rules of competition for whatever arena you happen to be in. It's also knowing the business of your business, whether your business is playing basketball like Coach Wooden, leading troops in battle like Richard Winters and Jim Mattis, or leading people in a giant corporation like Indra Nooyi. It's teaching your team to correctly put on their shoes and socks so that nothing that they can control gets in the way of them being the best that they can be.

Richard Winters and Jim Mattis are good examples of what it takes. Both were wartime leaders who took the unusual step (one the accepted leaders did not take) of learning as much as they possibly could about how to win a battle with the least possible loss of troops *before* they ever went into battle. In a similar vein, Coach John Wooden competed in the game of basketball, but he was far more than a student of the game. He was its preeminent scholar, studying how the game was played and won, and how it evolved over time as the nature of his team members evolved. The same sort of challenge exists for you and your team. It may be hard to hear, but if you're not a student of what you do, you will never excel at it, whether it is golf, restaurateurship, medicine, stamp collecting, fly fishing, or leadership.

You have to know the business of your business, as well as how to lead people. As an example of knowing the business of your business, a good friend of mine—Jack Suarez of Homebuilding Partners, Inc.—is a fourth-generation home-builder. He has built thousands of homes and often makes the point that you actually have to know how to build a home in order to build a good one *and* understand what it means to the homeowner to own one. He makes the point in one of his company's four cornerstones:

> *A Beautiful Home Built to Last:* Building a home to high standards in a community where people want to live and that has terrific curb appeal, popular options and design traditions, and provides a pleasurable home ownership experience. *It is a best-in-class home for the money.*[2]

It's clear from this cornerstone that Jack means not only the physical process of construction, but also site selection, design, and understanding the emotional aspects of home ownership. This kind of deep knowledge is part of establishing your credibility as a leader and your ability to make a difference in the lives of others. Go for it, and please accept what follows as icing on the cake of learning the business of your business.

WINNERS CREATE WINNERS

What do Jon Stewart, Marisa Mayer, the late Norman Brinker, and Lorne Michaels have in common? Although they span a wide range of years, industries, and diverse political perspectives, all of them created actively loyal and high-performance teams that enabled their members to grow and excel in their own right. This latter aspect—*excel in their own right*—is a critical part of making a difference in the lives of others.

Between them, Lorne Michaels and Jon Stewart incubated the talents of Steve Carrell, Tina Fey, Seth Meyers, Stephen Colbert, and Maya Rudolph, among others. While Marisa Mayer was at Google, she led teams that included the current Salesforce president Bret Taylor, and the founder of the successful millennial-focused media company Brit + Co, Brit Morin. Norman Brinker's leader-incubator produced Chris Sullivan (Outback Steakhouse), Hal Smith (Hal Smith Restaurant Group), Dick Rivera (chairman of National Restaurant Association), George Biel (Hillstone Restaurant Group), Dick Frank (Chuck E. Cheese), Mike O'Donnell (Ruth's Chris Steak House), and Jeff Shearer (Blockbuster Video, Boston Market, Lost Dunes Golf Club, and Ditka's Restaurant Group), among others.

The Principles of Success

Each of these leaders did what Coach Wooden did: *prepare to compete.* It's certainly no surprise that the best-prepared team is most often the winning team. I like sports, but I'm not a sports nut. When I watch sports it's mostly college teams in the major sports, like football and basketball (Go Badgers!). I also watch minor sports, like volleyball, baseball, and college wrestling, and have noticed something about successful teams regardless of whether it's a major or minor sport:

1. The same teams tend to be in the running for the national championship year after year.

2. The teams that win national championships have the best players.

3. The winning teams retain their leaders.

That last observation—*leaders who stay*—is likely the primary source of the first two characteristics—*in any form of competition*. In the major college sports, like basketball and football, elite players churn much faster than they do in Division II or Division III schools and, hopefully, your business. Indeed, it's close to a 100 percent turnover, with college basketball being famous for "one and done" superstars. The best players leave to take advantage of the opportunity to earn big bucks in professional basketball as soon as the end of their freshman year. So how do the best coaches win despite losing their best players year after year? In addition to staying, winning coaches follow three principles:

1. **Make winning a team tradition:** the expectation of working hard within the team and against other teams is clear to team members *before* they join the team.

2. **Winners want to be on winning teams:** A-Players are drawn to hard work and want to play with and compete against other A-Players.

3. **Players fit the team's culture:** culture stays the same as players come and go.

With respect to the first principle, Adored Leaders quickly replace team members who can't or won't perform, thereby creating an opportunity for new team members and increasing the likelihood of a winning team. The second principle builds on the first one and points to the importance of building a track record of success. A-Players like to compete with other A-Players. In terms of the third principle, you might think that team member churn would prevent perennial winners like Nick Saban (Alabama), Mike Krzyzewski (Duke), and Paul Chryst (Wisconsin) from repeat championships, but it doesn't. That's because these *leaders stay and build the team's culture and only recruit players who fit it.*

There is a major point here: *the right culture is a key (perhaps, even the key) to any team's success.* For example, have you noticed that it's not always the team with the best players that wins? More often than not, it's the team with the best teamwork. That's why I believe that culture-building is a leader's most important responsibility, followed by staffing it with team members who perform, fit, and stay. Your takeaway from this riff is this: learn what a culture is and how one is built, as culture-building is a skill like most other things when it comes to leadership. In fact, I would go so far as to say that everything you do as a leader is in support of a high-performance culture, one with the right language, right morality, and right rules (chapter 1).

In support of this conclusion, it has been my experience that the higher a team is in a company's hierarchy (e.g., the executive team), the more likely it is for one of its team members to be replaced because he or she doesn't fit the team's culture than for any other reason, including performance. That's far less true in sports, simply because only A-Players who fit the team's culture are invited to join the team in the first place, and if they don't work out, they don't play. It also helps that athletes seek out teams where they believe they will have the best opportunity to fit in, play, and thrive.

A DEEPER DIVE INTO THE FIVE QUESTIONS

If these three principles are valid, the question is this: What do you need to know about leading people beyond what you have already learned from the prior chapters? What follows are a few things that

I have seen enough times to conclude that they are crucial to creating a high-performance culture; indeed, they just might be the difference-makers in your success.

Remember the five questions that team members ask their leaders to answer? (For your convenience, I'll repeat them here.) Team members want to know the following:

1. Where are we going?

2. What will it be like when we get there?

3. How will we get there?

4. Can you get us there?

5. What's in it for me?

That's pretty much the whole ball of wax: if your leadership provides positive answers to each of these questions, your team members have a positive team experience and, voilà, your team is successful. It should not go without saying that the words and actions of Adored Leaders are compelling answers to these questions that *earn the active loyalty of your team members and turn them into a high-performance team* (my definition of a leader again). While keeping the four promises to team members (chapter 6) is the primary method of answering the questions, there's something more to being an Adored Leader than that.

Part of that something lives inside of you, in how you answer really hard questions like "Why am I here, and what difference does it make?" What I am talking about is no less than your *life purpose*, core beliefs about success, and what you think it takes to compete within the arena you are in—retail, health care, manufacturing, nongovernmental organizations, you name it. Another part lives in your team's environment, in how you understand the *basics* of your team's success.

Something I Can Love

I have been using "making a difference in the lives of others" as the driving force in the life of an Adored Leader. But what is this force, and why is it so important to your personal growth? I don't want to go all mystical on you, and have worked really hard in the pages up to this one to stay in the here and now with immediately useful hacks on how to improve your leadership.

However, there comes a time when it's absolutely necessary for you to challenge the magic between your ears, or you will not grow. You'll certainly be a better leader, but you will not cross the finish line to being an Adored Leader. That requires you to step from your Zone of Comfort to your Zone of Challenge.

Hopefully, I can rev you up with a bit of a sales pitch. When you have a driving sense of purpose, you rarely start your day wondering what you're going to do. I've seen this in action. I live in "Olympic City, USA" (aka Colorado Springs). Early one morning last spring I was driving down a long road near my home. Off in the distance, a runner was coming toward me. I didn't know who he was, but I could tell that he could run like few others can. I'd never seen anyone run that fast, except on TV. That, despite a pouring rain, temperature in the low 40s, and being at least ten miles from the Olympic Training Center. Water was splashing every time he put his foot down, but his body was perfectly relaxed and still except for the smooth action of his arms and the powerful drive of his legs. As he came closer, I recognized him as one of the distance runners I had seen on TV—I have no idea which one. It made me wonder how often he did this very same run—rain, snow, or sunshine—and for how many years he had been doing it. You don't pay the price he paid for his excellence without having a purpose.

While not all of us are driven to be a world champion, all of us are capable of doing more through purpose. When you are chasing your purpose, you are automatically energized and focused and your life is easier and less stressful. You have something to do that is meaningful to you. Elon Musk is a prime example of the energy inherent in purpose. The multibillionaire founder of Tesla was asked during the ramp-up to production of the new Model 3 in 2019 what it was that energized his 120-hour workweeks.

> The fundamental goodness of Tesla . . . so like the "why" of Tesla, the relevance . . . comes down to two things: acceleration of sustainable energy and autonomy. . . . The acceleration of sustainable energy is absolutely fundamental, because this is the next potential risk for humanity. . . . But autonomous cars have the potential to save millions of lives . . . so that is critical.[3]

This driving force has served to set Tesla—and Musk—apart from the competition. In fact, if you look at consumer preferences when it comes to electric vehicles, it's no accident that Tesla has no competition. Nor is it a surprise that Musk has shared the battery technology of his company—for free.

This focused nature of a purpose-driven life has led me to wonder if what we call "multitasking" isn't simply an excuse for lack of purpose. That is, do people work on many things because there is no one thing that commands their attention? As I look back on my own experience, a lack of a clear purpose in my life nicely explains my tendency, particularly early in my life, to be easily bored, lose focus, and go through occasional bouts of anxiety. I found my purpose in teaching.

I count myself among those leaders who are not all that good at cause-finding or identifying a unifying purpose for their team to commit to. But the importance of doing it anyway is the point Meg Whitman made in her book *The Power of Many: Values for Success in Business and in Life*: "Success happens when good people with good intentions cooperate and work together over a shared interest."[4] She's correct, and the fact that many teams and enterprises are not inspiring does not mean that they can't be.

Purpose is something that drives you toward a fulfilling future. A company can have a purpose, a team can have a purpose, and individuals can have a purpose. The power to make a difference comes from the *alignment* of these perspectives of company, team, and individual into a unifying cause. As an example, Mission BBQ puts its purpose front and center on its website:

> Our young men and women in uniform. Veterans who served with honor. Our local Police, Firefighters and First Responders who make Our Community a better place to live. They're the people who we respect most of all, so Mission BBQ tries to give back [to them] in return.[5]

So how does this purpose translate into action for Mission BBQ and its team members? Restaurant teams stop operations to salute the flag at noon every day as a symbol of this purpose, support several military-based charities with fundraisers, and provide discounts to first responders. The tangible result is more than eleven million dollars in donations to related charities since opening its doors in 2011.[6] That's a team putting its money where its heart is. As a bonus, for the people who align with this purpose, Mission BBQ adds value to their employment and customer experiences that goes beyond having a job or meal, respectively, to providing an emotional connection and the pride of being part of something bigger than themselves. Mission BBQ is an example of a grand purpose that suffuses an entire company with energy from top to bottom to be shared with its vendors, customers, and community.

However, your purpose does not need to be this grand. Coach John Wooden defined his own purpose as a young man before starting his professional life and made it the core of his achievement as both an athlete and a coach. His purpose was *preparation and teamwork—perfectly executed.* In this light, basketball was only a vehicle for his larger life purpose, something that gave his time on earth a meaning that he valued. Importantly, Coach didn't insist that his team win, only that it compete at the highest level achievable as a team and that there be no regrets, win or lose. (Remember, each season began with how to put on socks and properly lace up a pair of sneakers.) It's this personal perspective that makes purpose so powerful and, when shared, results in team cohesion and an elevated level of performance. Always.

Although a thorough discussion of your search for meaning and purpose is beyond the scope of this book, there are some things that you can do in order to get yourself started. A question that I have found useful in this effort is a simple one: What do you want your legacy to be? Answering this question makes you think of what you want to accomplish with your life. You can follow this question with a series of "why" questions. For example, let's imagine that you answer the question with "I want to be a good person." Good purpose, but kind of broad. So you ask, "Why do I want to be a good person?" and you answer, "Because good people go to heaven"; you respond with "Why do good people go to heaven?" and you answer, "Because they make a difference"; you ask, "Why do they make a difference?" and you answer, "Because the people they touch have a better life"; and so forth. Notice that with this technique you get very specific very fast, as in when you ask, "Why do they have a better life?" and you answer, "Because I have taught them something that they can use." However you go about it, pursuing these meaning-of-life sorts of questions is useful and can be life-changing.

The examples of purpose illustrate the importance of you establishing a purpose for yourself and infusing it into your team. By doing so, you answer the second and fifth question of the five asked by your A-Players in a way that builds their sense of belonging, significance, and pride. I'd go so far as to say that given the power of purpose to motivate team members and sustain a high level of performance, failure to establish an inspiring purpose for your team is tantamount to condemning it to mediocrity.

How Not to Die

A competitive key is something that has to be in place in order for a team to have any hope of being successful. Every industry has them: some are unique to a particular industry, while others generalize across several industries. During my work with leaders over the years, it has become obvious that these keys are frequently only recognized in a foggy sort of way.

I see that fog in the use of terms like "innovation," "engineering," "service," and "technical know-how." Foggy thinking results in the proliferation of feel-good statements like "exceed expectations," "the brand," and "customer centricity," while adding nothing to your team's ability to compete. One of the things I like about a fully articulated competitive key is how it helps to answer the first question ("Where are we going?"), as well as the third question ("How will we get there?").

Based on the nature of the competitive landscape in major collegiate sports, I'd hazard a guess that one of the competitive keys is not what you might suspect (i.e., get the best players). Rather, it's this: make sure you recruit, nurture, and keep the right coach. It's the coach who builds the right culture and recruits A-Players who fit it. If I'm correct (and I'm just guessing here), it would not be a surprise if the best athlete isn't sometimes passed over for one with less athletic ability, but who has values that better align with the team's culture. In short, the right leader facilitates the right culture and team members.

Obviously, I don't know all industries, but I do know that for many, quality employees are seen as a competitive key. However, in my view that perspective is one level down from where it should be focused. For any enterprise in the service business—whether a restaurant, hotel, health care, banking, or retail store—it's true that you are no better than the ability of customer contact employees to execute the intended customer, client, guest, or patient experience. That source of competitive edge is facilitated not by focusing on customer contact employees, but focusing on their leader(s) as *the* competitive key. I call it *Stable Quality Management at the unit level (SQM)*. These are managers who stay, get very good at their jobs, and build connections with team members so that they can build connections with customers.

What SQM enables is this: *the faces, hearts, and hands of the customer experience.* These are frontline and hourly employees who get good at their jobs, know the customers and their quirks, *and* stay. It's an *enabled* competitive key, and I call it being *fully staffed with fully trained employees.* When management turnover is high, employee turnover will also be high, customer frequency low, and social media ratings dismal. It's that complex organization thing again. This relationship between team member stability and the active loyalty of customers is what makes the acceptance of high management turnover so hard to understand. It's stupid, and it's poor leadership to boot.

One way to get a handle on your team's competitive key(s) is to take a hard look at your team's pain points. It's a good idea to start this inspection at the business unit level, such as with a department, individual store, health care facility, branch office, or restaurant. I'd also recommend that you do it by talking to real team members in each unit, rather than doing it as an abstract exercise by a higher-level task force. This way, you will get multiple points of view and, where the viewpoints converge, you will find a competitive key. Once identified, call a "911 meeting" and figure out what to do about it. What you will find is that all of this homework pays off in the form of a straightforward action plan.

Where'd I Put Them?

I can never find my reading glasses, so I buy cheap ones in bunches and leave them all over the house and stash several pairs in my study—where I still can't find them! It would be cheaper for me to simply remember where I put my glasses, but that would require that I establish a new habit. By default, I've decided that it's easier—not cheaper—to carelessly stage them everywhere I might need a pair of readers and then, hopefully, be able to find one of my staging areas.

Company leaders often can't find their "reading glasses" or, what I call, their business basics. I have worked with several turnaround situations in my career. One of the things I can count on is that the new leadership team (or the old one, if they have had reality therapy but were left in place) seeks to "get back to basics." This sounds like a good idea, but, like my reading glasses, you have to remember where you put them.

It always reminds me of what my dad would say after he screwed something up: "I wonder if reading the instructions would have helped?" (He was a confident mechanic, so he didn't always take the time to read them.) But what if you can't find the instructions for your team's success? What if the basics of success have been lost to memory, as is often the case?

It's hard to get back to basics, simply because of the casual method by which they are developed. Rather than being consciously created, business basics typically slowly evolve over time through trial and error to become part of the company's DNA. This natural process leaves them below the level of conscious awareness.

I've seen this problem so many times that I have developed a simple method for recapturing them. But be careful, as the basics of building a team and the basics of success are not the same. Business basics are hard for a leadership team to identify in the abstract, so I give them a framework and an introduction that helps them to get granular that has four parts:

1. **People Basics:** things that have to be in place in terms of employees in order for them to take care of customers.

2. **Operating Basics:** things that have to be in place in order to consistently deliver the intended customer experience.

3. **Customer Basics:** things that compose the customer experience and affect the nature of their memory of the experience.

4. **Financial Basics:** things that have to be in place in order for the enterprise to thrive financially.

A part of the process is designed to help the team distinguish between a competitive key and a business basic. A broad-stroke difference is that competitive keys are worked on endlessly by team members at all levels in the enterprise, while business basics happen every day at the level of the business unit to ensure that customers profitably receive the intended customer experience. I'll use a detailed example to make my point.

At the founding of Outback Steakhouse in 1988, the founding team and I had a pivotal discussion. Lots of it dealt with cultural issues, in that it had to do with core beliefs about restaurant success. One of the beliefs held strongly by CEO Chris Sullivan was that "the best restaurants are local." That's it, and he would not accept any "Yeah, buts" to this belief. That led to an initial requirement that a restaurant's proprietor come from the local community. In terms of SQM, the discussion focused on how a proprietor could "act local"— that is, get to know her customers and their names and preferences, participate in community events, join local business groups, have skin in the game, and live near her restaurant. The discussion made SQM a strategic imperative: something that is complex, worked on all of the time at all levels and across all functions, measured, and rewarded. It's from this discussion that Outback's innovative "Proprietor Program" evolved and caught hold in order to grow the company.[7]

The detail of the program makes the depth of thought behind it clear. The proprietor of an Outback Steakhouse bought and owned a percentage of the business, had his or her name over the door, and could not transfer to another Outback that might be better. Instead, the proprietor was treated like an owner in that he or she had to make the restaurant successful or fail. The proprietor committed to a five-year contract with a big financial payout at the end *if* he or she built the business, received a distribution of 10 percent of cash flow, and so on. On top of that, as the company grew, more and more of the proprietors came from the hourly ranks of Outbackers, and therefore had to be developed and trained into an ownership role. It's an understatement that proprietorship was a very complex program that demanded the constant input of operations, finance, legal, and HR. All of it was based on a single belief: "All of the best restaurants are local." The program was effective enough that it governed the company's growth and dominated its culture for the first twenty years of the company's life and was discontinued in its original form only after the company was sold to Bain Capital.

Basics are simple: "Greet every patient and offer a refreshment." "Scrape the gum off the sidewalk." "Pick up all papers in the parking lot twice daily." "Vacuum all metal shavings in real time." "Cutting gloves are mandatory." "Be fully staffed." "Lock the back door." "Follow the hiring process." "Escort every customer to their car with an umbrella when raining." "A manager personally responds to every Yelp review with four stars or fewer." "Send some employees home when business is less than budgeted." "No overtime." "Rotate inventory daily." "If you're ordering supplies correctly, your shelves will be nearly empty the day before a delivery."

As you can see from these examples, business basics are the stuff of day-to-day taking care of business. There is nothing strategic about them, except their origin. If you have ever taken flying lessons or happen to notice what airline pilots do before takeoff, then you understand that basics are like a checklist that ensures that the team is ready to take care of business. Sometimes basics can get complex, as these two examples from BKS-Partners, Inc. (a risk-management and employee benefits company) illustrate:[8]

> **BKS 20:20:** Assessing oneself, each other and our teams in real time with thoughtful reflection and an honest critique of individual and team performance. *Looking back with our eyes wide open and a clear lens sharpens our skills and helps us make our way forward.*

Constant Improvement: Challenging ourselves to be the best through research, client listening, gathering industry intelligence, and systematically debriefing our failures. *Making excellence a defining quality of our culture.*

BKS-Partners' basics push the envelope on simplicity, but that's okay, as long as they are taught and followed by team members and fit the company's culture and business model. Contrast the BKS basics with a couple from Ruth's Chris Hospitality Group, Inc.:[9]

Quality: Consistently delivering the best steak house experience through adherence to industry-leading standards and procedures. *Quality is a source of our considerable pride in Ruth's Chris and one another.*

Fun: Bringing a sense of playfulness to what we do, being able to laugh at ourselves and letting the good times roll. *Fun is a source of the fond memories we create.*

Fiscal Responsibility: Achieving long-term success through a balanced approach to growing sales, managing costs, and earning a profit. We do not pinch the pennies, but we do count them in the context of their investment value for improving the experiences of *Our People. Fiscal Responsibility is a source of a future of which we can be proud.*

These examples are but a few of the total list of basics for each company. For both companies, the basics serve to focus day-to-day attention on what needs to be constantly done in order to succeed and to keep the business relevant to and resonant with their customers.

It's not so much that basics are part of the definition of an Adored Leader; instead, they facilitate earning the active loyalty of team members and molding them into a high-performance team. Whatever your sphere of responsibility—a work team, a business unit, or an entire company—there are basics to be identified, codified, and used. Basics are not something you get back to, but something you use to ensure that your team remains able to perform.

In this chapter I've added a few wrinkles that should ease your journey to being an Adored Leader. We have all heard it more than a few times, but things like aspirational goals, inspiring purpose, and business basics that work really do help you to focus on what's important—and get it done. I find things like these, especially goals and purpose, have a wonderful way of focusing your thoughts and actions on your challenges, opportunities, and team members. In the final chapter, I will throw in a few final thoughts about the nature of Adored Leadership.

LEADER TO-DO LIST

- ☐ What are you currently doing that tells you that you are providing good answers to your team's five questions?
- ☐ What is the competitive key for your team?
- ☐ What do you have in place that ensures your competitive key is strong?
- ☐ What do you need to put in place in order to strengthen your competitive key?
- ☐ What are the business basics for your team?
- ☐ How do you use the basics with your team?

10

LEADING WITH NO REGRETS

BRINGING IT ALL TOGETHER

What you do makes a difference, but it's up to you
to decide what that difference will be.

I introduced my dad in an earlier chapter, noting his habit of making two of everything when it was reasonable to do so. When I first read about Coach John Wooden's insistence on wrinkle-free socks and his personal philosophy of superb preparation to compete, it naturally reminded me of my dad. Both of them loved to prepare and neither left performance to chance. My dad was the king of checklists, studied directions (usually), loved procedures, and worked to a principle of excellence that many craftsmen follow to this day: "Measure twice, cut once." My dad and Coach Wooden knew something about excellence that will serve you well on your journey to being an Adored Leader. That something is preparation and a watchmaker's eye for detail.

GET READY TO BUILD

Becoming an Adored Leader requires that you *use your head before you use your hands* and *practice until you get things right.* That's what Will Durant had in mind with his quip that *excellence is a habit*—and it's also a three-step process:

1. **Think** about what it is you want to accomplish in detailed (and, hopefully, measurable) terms.

2. **Visualize** how you will accomplish it in a step-by-step manner: this first, then this, and so on.

3. **Reflect** on what went well and what you could have done better, with raising the bar in mind.

This is no different than the process that world-class athletes follow in order to achieve their personal best today, new personal best tomorrow, and world record the day after that. It works for them, and it will work for you.

As noted in the last chapter, the process requires that you *step from your Zone of Comfort to your Zone of Challenge.* If that's not something you are willing to do on a regular basis, then you will not grow. As Ginni Rometty (former CEO at IBM) says, "Growth and comfort do not coexist." So get comfortable with being uncomfortable.

There is no other way you will grow into living by a challenging code of honor, achieving all that it is possible for you to achieve, and making a difference in the lives of others. It's one of the hardest things you will ever do, but if being an Adored Leader is your goal, you'll have to develop an attitude of insisting upon the best from yourself today—and a bit better tomorrow.

If you choose to make the journey that becoming an Adored Leader requires, there are *values* you have to consider, *principles* you have to follow, and *habits* you'll need to develop to move you along your path. Much of what you need in order to step on the path was introduced in the first nine chapters. This chapter dips a toe into some of the challenges you'll face along the way and provides a useful summary of your journey to being an Adored Leader.

Can You Pass the Test?

The test of leadership is the presence of followers. What that means is that you have to lead before your followers can follow. That's a lot different than simply being in charge. The nature of the difference seems obvious until you stop and think about not only how rare Adored Leaders are, but also how rare Adored Followers are. Speaking personally, I can count on one hand the number of Adored Leaders I have had in my life and still have some fingers left over. Having said that, it may well be that the scarcity of Adored Leaders explains, in large part, the scarcity of Adored Followers.

We've all been on teams where the poor performance of a few team members cost you some wins and, even worse, sucked the spirit out of the team. They were an absolute pain in the ass to everyone, including themselves. The A-Players would get upset and wonder why the leader didn't do something about it, and when nothing was done, they'd often vote no on the team with their feet.

Alternatively, recall what happens when you make the call on a subpar team member? All of a sudden, the team's morale spikes up—and all you did was what you should have done in the first place.

One of the things I can tell you from personal experience is that the leader is often the last to know about problem team members.

We had a team member who was addicted to pain pills. At the time I did not know much about addiction, so I missed the clues. One of the things he would do is to injure himself so that he had to go to the emergency room to get treatment, resulting in another prescription for painkillers. Me? I just thought he was a klutz or had some kind of weird fascination with scars. Another clue was how easily he became angry when he needed a pill or two. He'd explode, insult his teammates, and, worse yet, harass them.

He never showed any of these behaviors in front of me. Looking back, I probably should have been suspicious, if only because he was so deferential to me. I'm not charming enough that anyone should be as deferential toward me as he was. To make a long story just a bit longer, my partner and I didn't know any of this until one of our teammates told us about him harassing and intimidating her while they were traveling together on business. That incident immediately ended his time with us and taught us a lesson that can serve you well: *the relationship you have with your team is never as transparent as you think it is.*

On a similar note, when a team is off track, it's the rare leader who can recognize that the problem is the leader and not the team members. The most common problem I see in the behavior of the leaders I have worked with sounds small, but has a huge effect on team morale and performance. It's the lack of consistent and predictable behavior on the part of the leader. Leaders are often inconsistent when it comes to keeping the four promises of *Clear Direction, Preparation, Support,* and *You Count* to team members, or unpredictable in terms of how they handle a given situation. If you're a leader whose team members have to find the right time to approach you, you're an inconsistent and unpredictable leader.

Inconsistency and unpredictability are only part of the problem. The other part is tolerating team members who should not have been on the team in the first place, like my drug-addicted team member. Most of us have been in this situation and later wondered why we did not take action. Good question, because as I said earlier, every time I have ever terminated a problem team member, the morale of the team magically and immediately went up. Every single time!

The reality is that it's easier to keep a marginal team member than it is to go through the hassle of hiring and training a new one. That's especially true in a time of full employment. But I'd have to say, in defense of myself and other leaders, that I don't believe it's usually a conscious decision to keep marginal team members, as it's simply the easiest path to follow. And try as we may to be disciplined, we are hardwired to take the path of least resistance. That wiring is one of the reasons there are so few Adored Leaders.

TRUST ONLY THE TRUSTWORTHY

Trust has been an implicit part of the conversation up to now, but I would like to make it explicit. First, by defining it: *trust is coming through in any situation requiring judgment, discretion, performance, and results.* You should write this definition down, memorize it, and make it your own. Why? Because trust is the central element of the relationship between any leader and his or her team. Not only that; it also starts not with the team member, but with the leader. In short, you have to first be trustworthy before I will trust you to lead me. Sounds like a circular argument, but it isn't. It's why *it's you, and not your team members, who is on probation.* This order of trust from leader to follower is evident in the story of Richard Winters in the introduction to this book, but it's even more obvious in Doris Kearns Goodwin's history of Abraham Lincoln's rise to the presidency.[1] It's one of the best books ever on the power of an Adored Leader to earn the active loyalty of team members and mold them into a high-performance team.

Both Major Winters and President Lincoln *earned* the adoration of their followers by *committing* themselves to two things: first, to the team's mission and second, to the team members themselves. It was the biography of Lincoln that cemented my belief that the leader's character drives everything the team achieves—or does not achieve. "Honest Abe" was not a PR label for Lincoln; rather, it was an accurate summary of his character and how he earned the loyalty of his cabinet members, despite the fact that each and every one of them thought him a rube and held him in contempt when he first came to office. By the time of his assassination, with the exception of one member of his cabinet, all of them would have taken a bullet for him—he was a trusted and truly Adored Leader. I like pictures, so let me show you what the process of earning the trust (and active loyalty) of team members looks like, regardless of whether you are an Abraham Lincoln or any other Adored Leader. I call it the Trust Equation:

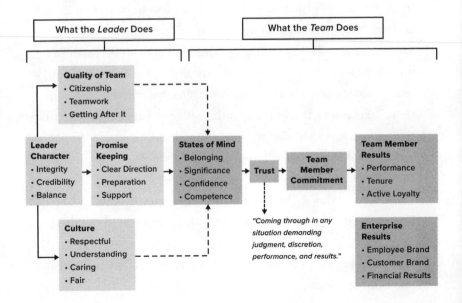

The Trust Equation

The first thing to notice about the Trust Equation is that everything in it is within your direct or indirect control. The action areas in gray are under your direct control, starting with your personal character. Character determines the nature of the team members you recruit and, more importantly, the nature of the team members you retain on your team. Culture is shown in its narrowest sense as the tone of the relationships among team members (an aspect of the culture's morality). It is you who builds and protects the team's culture. Finally, there are the generic promises you keep to your team members.

It's what you say and do in your areas of action that influence the States of Mind of your team members (along with the values and beliefs that they bring to the team). The five states of mind determine whether you are trusted—that is, whether you come through in situations demanding discretion, judgment, performance, and results. In short, this is your team's perception of your trustworthiness. From this flows all of the good things that you want from having given your team members what *they* want—namely, commitment, an actively loyal and high-performing team—and the results expected of you as a team leader: positive employee and customer brands and financial results. This flow from you to your team members to positive outcomes makes becoming an Adored Leader not easy, but a pretty straightforward process of preparation, practice, and growth.

KEEPING YOUR EYES ON THE PRIZE

Sometimes you don't know that you're being prepared to lead, but it is preparation nonetheless. I worked one summer for the US Forest

Service as a firefighter in the High Sierras on the border between California and Nevada. It was a beautiful place and should have turned into an "every summer" job, but it didn't. I like to hike (we did lots of that) and go fly-fishing (there are streams everywhere), and fighting fires is exciting (and extremely hard) work. It was the whole ball of wax outdoors-wise, but I decided not to sign up for the next summer. It wasn't the work—I liked it—but rather the dogmatic leadership, and I was probably too young to just let it roll off my back. Or, just maybe, it was the contrast with another guy I had worked for.

Bill DuBois was a Chevron dealer in my neighborhood. I worked nights and weekends in his gas station during high school in the off-season. During my sophomore year working for Bill, I sold a set of new tires to a customer. That's the good news. The bad news is that I had screwed up and charged the wholesale rather than the retail price. I'm sure we had one happy customer. As for me, I was so excited about making my first sale that I didn't notice my mistake. We had sold and installed a lot of tires that Saturday, so no one noticed my error until Bill was tallying up the day's sales, and, of course, the customer was long gone.

Bill was very direct with me. He asked how the mistake happened. I really didn't have an explanation except the obvious one: I looked at the wrong column of numbers and quoted the customer the wholesale price. Bill had a tendency to go red in the face when he was upset. So it didn't surprise me that he was bright red as he reminded me that selling tires at a loss was not a good business practice. Bill never raised his voice or belittled me for my mistake; instead, he came up with a solution that probably wouldn't fly today—I would pay the difference between the wholesale and retail price out of my wages.

What he did taught me a valuable lesson about paying attention to details, but what he did not do is even more important from a leadership perspective. He protected my dignity by not mentioning my mistake in front of the other team members, nor did he ever mention the incident again, ever—and I never made the same mistake on any product, including tires, again. As a fifteen-year-old boy, I had learned a ton about leadership, accountability, and caring from Bill that I really only appreciated later in life. I'd have to say that Bill was my first Adored Leader, and, while I did not like the process of being held accountable, I loved the result: I was prepared for more responsibility.

Where all this brings me to is this: *the excellence embodied in being an Adored Leader is recognized and rewarded by the team member rather than the leader.* In short, *it is earned*—and you may never even hear about it until years later, if ever. I, for example, never told Bill how much I appreciated what he taught me. What he taught me is embodied in the Trust Equation. If you're lucky, some of your team members will tell you how much of a difference you've made in their lives, but most won't. However, if you follow the equation, you'll know without being told. In the equation, the box labeled Leader Character is from the Honor Pyramid presented in chapter 4. I encourage you to think of the boundaries as the price of admission to being an Adored Leader.

I recently witnessed the downside of the Honor Pyramid when I spent some time with the CEO of a company and his team. According to the CEO, "the wheels were wobbling on the company," while his team described the company as "chaotic." I didn't spend enough time with him to say whether the CEO had integrity and balance, but I did spend enough time with his team to understand that he had no credibility with them. He had the worst form of "leader-itis": he was judged to be incompetent and seen as lacking the personal insight to admit that he was in over his head and the wisdom to ask his team for help. He wasn't doing well with *his* part of the Trust Equation, and therefore was not seen as trustworthy.

A TINY BIT OF PSYCHOLOGY

In a healthy person, values drive behavior—your words and actions. Behavior is the bottom line of character as it's really the only way that anyone, including your team members, has any idea of what you stand for. Psychology is the science of understanding and predicting human behavior and identifying the values that drive it. That makes it an endlessly fascinating topic. My interest in the topic is what is called positive psychology. Briefly, in contrast to the traditional illness model of psychology, positive psychology is concerned with understanding the mechanism by which people flourish and, from there, figuring out how to translate that understanding into behavior change strategies. An important cornerstone of positive psychology is the assumption that flourishing is largely determined by the choices a person makes in the big and little things of life.

Why people make the choices they do is a long-term interest of mine. It includes understanding why people choose to do things that are bad for them, as well as why they choose to serve others. For example, why do a few young Americans choose to join the military each year, knowingly at the risk of their lives? It's an interesting question in light of the fact that in today's social environment, they can easily avoid military service without judgment. Or, why do leaders choose to be *accepted* when they could be *adored*? That's a question I have tried to answer for a long time, and a big part of my motivation for writing this book.

My key assumption in putting together my model of Adored Leadership is that leadership is a *choice* to make a difference in the lives of others, including oneself. That makes it about character and its two defining aspects: human goodness *and* achievement. Unless you stand for both, you won't be an Adored Leader. There are lots of examples of leaders who achieved much but are poor examples of human goodness. Some of them demonstrated outstanding personal competence, like Bernie Madoff and Jeffrey Epstein, but I can't think of anyone who would describe them as making a positive difference in the lives of others. When I am feeling a bit cynical, examples such as these are why I'm inclined to believe that talent, competence, and grit may well be all it takes to be a high achiever.

Achieving results is a big deal, but it's not honorable character. If you doubt that, think about a leader on the world stage who has talent, competence, and grit but who seems to operate in a world dedicated to themselves and their personal agenda. The point of all this is that *character has to be important to you beyond whatever else you personally achieve, or it will not be a part of who you are.* That's true if for no other reason than it takes way too much effort and personal sacrifice to get there. Hopefully, this riff on character has given you food for thought and will cause you to set a higher standard for your leadership than you might otherwise have done. If I have been successful, you will consciously add human goodness to whatever you aspire to be.

Good Questions—Not Often Answered

Facebook recently announced that it will not censor political ads.[2] It caused a firestorm. Twitter followed suit by announcing that it will not allow political ads.[3] That announcement caused only a few embers to fly. Which one is the right thing to do? As far as I can tell, the answer is, It depends. And the question is, It depends on what? That's a good question—not often asked and, less often, answered. In this case, it depends on who is losing their voice. In short, who wins and who loses by decisions such as these? What I can tell you is that if President Trump had not been in the White House, the question likely would have never come up.

Have you ever wondered what it means to be a grownup? Often the word used is "adult," but that has more to do with chronological age than with wisdom. I prefer the term "mature," as it implies some sort of emotional and moral arrival. It's November 7, 2019, as I'm drafting this chapter. There is snow on the ground, but it will be sunny and warm tomorrow; the unemployment rate in the county where I live is 3.5 percent; 750,000 people were killed in the genocide in Rwanda in the mid-1990s; three women and six children were murdered in Mexico last week; and two new restaurants are about to open within a mile of my home. These are eight facts of equal weight—that is, right up to the moment you overlay these facts with your sense of right and wrong.

So I'm not surprised when you say, "Tom. Wait a minute. The date and the weather mean very little. Who cares if it snowed last night? And the unemployment rate is a sign of the times. (If you had written this in 2009, the unemployment rate would have been more than twice as high.) But Rwanda was a real tragedy and smear on the face of humanity, as was the murder of those women and children." We are both correct, but for different reasons.

Differences in values among people are often the source of "it depends." I stated the facts as facts, free of my judgment of them, but you unavoidably read them in the context of your values. The talking heads I see on television rarely talk about facts; rather, they overlay them with their values, which turns them into different facts that better fit their perspective. My point: *facts have absolutely no importance without the meaning established by values.* In a team, it's the leader who determines the team's values and morality—and therefore the weight that will be put on the facts.

Values are often more important than the facts as they constitute the "should have been" of humanity that gives life its meaning. Thus, we say that the genocide in Rwanda "should have been" stopped, and that the murder of innocents is wrong, and humankind is made less by its happening. That's why President Bill Clinton said that the single largest regret from his time in office was that his administration did nothing to stop the genocide in Rwanda.[4] It wasn't the scandals he was involved in, it wasn't the tech bubble created on his watch, and it wasn't the economy. Taken at his word, it was a lapse in his humanity that he regretted the most, as he had given up the moral high ground.

COLORING YOUR FACTS

What does this discussion of the effect of your values on "the facts" have to do with you being an Adored Leader? In one word: *everything*. That's because the facts you pay attention to—and, more accurately, how you pay attention to them—are determined by your values. In this light, the decisions you make every day as a leader are not determined by the facts alone, but by how your values color the facts. In effect, your values—your take on human goodness—create their own reality. It is this reality within which you lead.

As a leader, when you give up the moral high ground, you lose everything that makes you worth trusting, as you have lost your right to say, "This is the right thing to do, and that's why we're doing it." Strong personal values are implicit in the actions of all Adored Leaders. That has made me wonder whether there is a common set of core values that anchor Adored Leaders and determine how they look at the facts of a situation. The short answer to that question is "Yes."[5]

You can learn a lot about the pattern of values—that is, human goodness—from reading philosophy,[6] as well as the biographies of leaders recognized by history as *consciously* having made a positive difference in the lives of others. Reading these stories of Adored Leaders allows you to see values in action.

The idea of values dates back more than 2,500 years to Greek and Roman philosophical discussions of virtue. To these ancient thinkers, virtue described the defining excellence of an object (or person) without regard to the morality of its use. Thus, the virtue of a knife is to cut, regardless of whether the cut was made to end or to save lives.

Over time, virtue took on a much more limited meaning having to do with *acting in the interest of others,* and to the use of the term "values" rather than "virtues." This modern context—and the well-documented fact that trust in leaders is at an all-time low— makes understanding what it means to be a values-based leader and to act with goodness an important aspect of your thinking as a leader.

The Big Six

There is a long and, for people driven to contemplating their navel, huge history of discussion about whether there is a core set of values. This discussion takes on heightened relevance when you start to ask whether there is a common set of values that cuts across all cultures, religions, and political beliefs to define our capacity for human goodness in any context, including leadership. The answer to this question is "mostly there is," as defined by six universal values.[7]

THE SIX CORE VALUES

Wisdom: Effective use of knowledge and experience; understanding or discernment of what is true, right, or lasting; being open to experience, inquisitive and insightful, thinking long term, exercising sound judgment, and being able to distinguish between symptoms and their underlying problems.

Courage: Facing threats and managing change with self-possession and resolution; being forthright, truthful, and honest, particularly when it would be easier not to and determined to be to be authentic.

Justice: Making an unfair world fairer; practicing moral rightness and being equitable in due process and the treatment of others.

Humanity: Seeing to the comfort and well-being of others; showing high concern for their dignity and being kind, generous, and compassionate.

Temperance: Having a balanced approach to life; practicing moderation and self-restraint; exercising caution and considering the consequences of words and actions.

Transcendence: Awareness that there is more to life than oneself; having a sense of purpose and appreciation for excellence and beauty, being optimistic, and working to make a difference in the lives of others.

The six core values define what it means to be a person defined by human goodness. There are a couple of things to know about the Big Six. First, within each one, individuals will differ in how they manifest the value. These are the individual's strengths of character and define his or her way of expressing the value. For example, some people manifest wisdom that has come to them largely through study and discussion, others through experience and practice, and still others by some combination of the two. Second, you do not have the luxury of choosing your favorite value or two, but have to be guided by all of them. This requirement of completeness is one reason that being a values-based person is so challenging and that Adored Leaders are so rare.

Being an Adored Leader is not about doing right in order to avoid the consequences of doing wrong. It's doing the right thing simply because it *is* right, even if it costs the team. From this perspective, *your values are not a means to an end; they are the end.* Thus, a little more concreteness can be added to the ideal of character. Specifically, living in accordance with a set of core values is a key to being an Adored Leader, as it does something that all followers crave: it makes you predictable, consistent, *and* likeable. It is this embracing of values-based behavior that serves to make your character the character of your team, and it's the same thing that draws them to your team.

"THE SECRET OF GETTING AHEAD IS GETTING STARTED"

Mark Twain hit the nail on the head with this particular bit of wit, as there is no question about having to step on the path to being an Adored Leader before you can be one. Reading this book is a first step on that path. You're stuck and destined to remain as you are *only* if you choose not to change it. Living a life of service to others is a skill, and, like all skills, it can be learned and will inevitably improve with practice.

Regardless of how much you practice, skills develop the fastest in the presence of clarity. That's the point behind Socrates's insight that "the beginning of wisdom is the definition of terms"—and it's the point of chapter 1, where you were asked to define a leader in a way that pleases you *and* is measurable. Another thing that needs defining is what you stand for. Hopefully, that little blurb about the Big Six values will be useful to you in that regard. Who are you, and what matters to you so much that you are willing to spend a lifetime pursuing it? In the lingo of personal development, it's called *values clarification*.

Next, make who you are clear to your team. That's setting standards, followed by constantly comparing your words and actions to your standard. In the lingo of leadership, this is called *clear direction*. Four questions that only you can answer about yourself will help you clarify you and your direction:

- Who are my heroes, and why are they my heroes?
- How do I want to be remembered by my team (my family, my friends, etc.)?
- What are the disciplines I need to develop in order to be remembered in that way?
- How can I keep myself honest to my personal vision moving forward?

This is a process of *conscious reflection*—in short, thinking about what you are about to do and what you just did in the context of the people you would like to be like. The Head, Heart, and Hand Triangle presented in the introduction to this book will help you to better understand the process. Whether you call it mindfulness, self-awareness, situational awareness, or something else entirely, it is the basic discipline of positive change and involves a cycle of learning, acting, and reflecting. In order to achieve the level of awareness that is characteristic of an Adored Leader, the process demands that you become a student of you!

It Really Is All About Me!

It has been my experience that many leaders know more about the company they work for than they do about themselves in terms of their dreams, goals, values, fears, strengths, and weaknesses. I have always thought it a mistake to keep yourself a mystery to yourself, but people do it all the time.

What is remarkable is that when they give this state of affairs some thought, people often consider the imbalance to be normal, or that it is simply too hard to think about all the "squishy stuff" of life. In the context of your personal development as a leader, normal is simply another word for accepted leader.

The Pyramid of Personal Character is a model that I use to help leaders move forward on the path to being an Adored Leader.

Pyramid of Personal Character

You likely remember this figure from chapter 4 and the discussion of honorable character. The difference here is that the source of the content of your character has to be detailed by you. The model is full of important terms, such as values, dreams, principles, commitments, disciplines, and results, each of which should be defined by you *in a way that is actionable.*

What are your values and dreams? By way of example, a goal is something that you shoot for, and good ones have certain qualities, such as being specific and measurable. For example, you might want to be a good parent to your children, or a good friend. These are admirable goals, but how will you know that you are making progress toward achieving them? It turns out that identifying indicators of success is one of the hard parts of being successful, but this is crucial to staying on track. That's why I wrote chapter 8. It may seem a quirky chapter in a philosophical book like this one, but lack of meaningful feedback is one reason why so many of our important goals get lost in the day-to-day of simply living.

That is especially true if your goal includes being an Adored Leader, as it's an easy one to lose sight of in the day-to-day hassles of leading a team. So keep your eye on the prize and look at sound indicators of progress like team member turnover, team member tenure, win-loss record, and percentage of team members who want to follow in your footsteps. It's the Team Member Egg all over again.

As you progress upward through the Pyramid of Personal Character, it evolves from the very abstract and conceptual—*values*—to the very observable and measurable—*results*—with each level—*disciplines, commitments, principles*—being more concrete than the one below it. Essentially, what you will be doing is creating your own vision or philosophy of life.

While the exercise is not all that hard in terms of clarifying the nature of the character you want to develop, turning clarity into disciplines and disciplines into habits of everyday behavior is very difficult. It seems as though nature is messing with us on this score, making it difficult to do the kinds of things that are good for us, like getting fit, eating right, studying, and reflecting on our journey; it is easy to do the stuff that is not so good for us. Fortunately, there has been a lot published lately about habit change. One of the more useful ones that I recently read is *Tiny Habits* by BJ Fogg.[8]

WHY BEING ADORED IS SO HARD

But the challenge of developing your character is not the only reason people do not make the journey to being an Adored Leader. For a long time, I was stumped about why it is that there are not more Adored Leaders. In the scheme of things, it's not any harder to do than a lot of other worthwhile pursuits. Besides that, it is emotionally rewarding for sure and can be very financially rewarding, too. So why wouldn't people as competitive as the average accepted leader strive to excel?

One of the reasons fueled the early years of my consulting practice: "It's lonely at the top." It's an absolutely true statement, even for the most transparent and open leader you can imagine. Many of the leaders I have worked with needed to have someone they could be candid with and who would be candid with them in return.

One of the seemingly weird things that I slowly learned from this experience at the tippy-top of leadership is that while it's hard to become an Adored Leader, it's even harder to stay that way. All of the Adored Leaders I have known had the triad of character—integrity, credibility, and balance—to begin with. For some, their *integrity* eroded with time and the weight of responsibility; others failed to keep up with the growth of their company or changes in its industry and lost *credibility*; and still others fell out of *balance*, often after taking their company public and adding the loudest stakeholder of all, stock analysts. From my vantage point on the sidelines, these slips and slides have been easy to see, but they are only symptoms of the problem. To understand the real problem, I had to go academic (again).

Abraham Maslow Was a Really Smart Guy

Toward the end of his life, the great psychologist, humanist, and philosopher Abraham Maslow (you may be familiar with him from having read about his needs hierarchy) posed a question: If self-actualization (the top of his hierarchy) or, as he called it, "achieving full humanness," is so compelling, why is it so rarely achieved? I was intrigued by the question because its answer has direct relevance to keeping an Adored Leader adored. While Maslow's answer to the question is challenging, it just might help you save yourself from your own nature:

> We fear our highest possibility . . . and are afraid to become [the person] we can glimpse in our most perfect moments. . . . We enjoy and even thrill to the . . . possibilities we see in ourselves . . . and simultaneously shiver with weakness, awe, and fear before these very same possibilities. . . . *We are just not strong enough to endure more [success] . . . [and] are just too weak for any large doses of greatness.* . . . For some people this evasion of one's own growth [through means such as] setting low levels of aspiration . . . are in fact defenses against grandiosity.[9]

Depending on your perspective, Maslow's answer is an obstacle to your growth or an opportunity to flourish by overcoming that obstacle. You pick: hang in there and stay on top of your game, or get there and cruise to an easier life.

If you see being an Adored Leader as an opportunity, then you have to actually learn how to handle accolades, visibility, and, very likely, being seen as arrogant by some people. For sure, you will be envied. Dealing with success is a skill at the heart of remaining successful! If you doubt that it's a skill, simply check the social media for athletes who have not learned to manage their success and compare them to those who have, like LeBron James, Tom Brady, and Justin Verlander.

THINK LIKE A BRAND

As a change of pace here, let's take a look at what you can learn from successful brands that could help you sustain yourself as an Adored Leader. As you might expect by now, I'll start the discussion with a definition of a brand: *a brand is the meaning derived from the experience of something* (such as a product or service). Mostly, we apply this definition to the customer's experience of a company's products and services, but there are many more ways to use it.

First, an experience is an experience, regardless of whether it's your customer or a team member having the experience. The content of the experiences is different, but *how the experience is processed to provide meaning is the same.* Second, a brand is a brand, regardless of whether it's your customer or leadership brand. *A strong brand symbolizes the connection between the customer (or team member) and your company (or you).* Thus, a good brand, like an Adored Leader, connects with the emotions of the stakeholder (customer or team member) to create fond memories. By the way, in both instances the memories created are built on—wait for it!— belonging and significance.

Where leaders go wrong is in promising more to their team members than it is possible to do, at least at a particular point in time. *It's not the experience but overpromising and underdelivering the experience that drives people nuts.* For example, being comfortable on a Southwest Airlines (SWA) flight is no more likely than being comfortable on any other airline. However, comfort is *not* what SWA promises its customers, nor does it try to allay their expectations of being uncomfortable. (Their leaders are too wise to make that promise.) Instead, the company simply says what it will do—*get you safely from where you are to where you want to go at an attractive price*—and, *sometimes, you will have fun.* That's the promise of SWA that leads to a key attribute of its brand: *honesty.* In short, SWA tells the truth about what it stands for, and so should you.

When your promises are clear and kept, it's fair to say that you have *integrity* and *credibility*. It's not a matter of wowing your team at all times; rather, it's a matter of being honest and predictable. Let's say you take over a failing team. It's a bad idea to promise the team that they will be hitting it out of the park tomorrow—but it would be a good idea to promise the team that the standards will be higher tomorrow on the way to turning things around. Integrity and credibility are as real as a sunrise or anything else that is a part of you; hence, it is important for your behavior to be consistent and predictable on the way to making the team a better team tomorrow than it is today.

Your Character Is a Brand, Only More Fragile

What should be apparent is that if you substitute the term "character" for the term "brand" in the preceding paragraphs, you could be talking about your team's experience of you. After all, *the experience provided by a leader creates meaning* and, in the instance of Adored Leaders like Richard Winters, Coach Wooden, and Indra Nooyi, it also results in fond memories. When I read the anecdotal description of these leaders by the people who had been on their respective teams, there was an undeniable sense that they were loved and valued. And those are two of the most important attributes of any brand!

Moreover, the same two qualities—relevance and resonance—determine whether you are adored and valued. *Relevance* is the question of whether you have good answers to your team's five questions (see chapter 6). *Resonance* answers the question of whether you are a positive force in the lives of your team members by meeting their needs for belonging and significance (chapter 2). So here is one more definition before I go: *an Adored Leader is someone who is a consistent source of relevant and resonant experiences to team members.*

By always working to be relevant and resonant, *you earn the active loyalty of people and mold them into a high-performance team.* Being adored is one of the many fond memories that your leadership brand can create. All it takes is for you to insist that you do some things differently, perhaps only a little bit different. At the end of the day, you're going to do what you're going to do—but it doesn't have to be what you have always done.

Welcome to the journey.

ACKNOWLEDGMENTS

Writing a book is an easier task than acknowledging who made the writing possible. While I was writing this book, I knew what I wanted to say, even if I stumbled from time to time on how to say it or said it badly. That's on me. But there were times in the writing process where I had to stop and think: *What's my point?* Thinking about "the point" often made me think about where I learned it.

Acknowledging where and from whom I had learned something was easy when the learning came from my habit of studying Adored Leaders in the abstract by reading their memoirs or the biographies written about them. This is impersonal learning at its best and really doesn't require any acknowledgment in a sense of having a debt of gratitude. Like many other authors, I have so deeply absorbed the lessons taught by Adored Leaders, like George Washington, Abraham Lincoln, Harriet Tubman, Eleonore Roosevelt, and Martin Luther King, Jr., that they have run together in my thinking to shape my core beliefs and principles.

The hard part is to acknowledge the personal lessons—that is, things I learned because someone took the time to teach me. In this book, I mention a few, like Bill DuBois from my gas station days, but there where many more going back to my childhood. My father's best friend, Gibby, is one of those. He was a very tall Cherokee Indian who grew up on a reservation and came of age during the Great Depression. Despite these strikes against him, he was a postcard for good-natured humor, patience, and wisdom shaped by difficult circumstances. He was a second father to me. His lesson was "Laugh, as this too shall pass." Then there were two police officers who were prominent throughout my upbringing from grade school through high school. They were twin brothers, and, for the life of me, I cannot remember their first names—likely, because I never used them. Both were "Officer Nettles" to me. They taught me that I could lead and about the importance of kindness.

In my academic career, there were two Adored Leaders: Dale Yoder and Ann Cleary. Dale painstakingly taught me how to write in a direct way, while Ann taught me how to think analytically and in terms of pictures. They both taught me to believe in myself and that I could do more than cut it in graduate school. Without Dale, I would not have gone to graduate school. Without Ann, I likely would never have finished.

My business career is studded with Adored Leaders. Carl Hays has been a "bestie" of mine for more than sixty years. He taught me that without mistakes, growth is not possible. He also taught me about accepting people as they are and that it is not my job to change them to fit my view of the world. Chris Sullivan was another of my Adored Leaders. While I am sure he did, I never saw him question his decisions or direction in public; he taught me the importance of certainty, standards, predictability, and an inspiring vision. Dick Rivera is another of my Adored Leaders. Dick can raise the mood and confidence of a group just by showing up. His was the lesson of positive spirit, can-do, and what he calls "gusto." Wyman Roberts rounds out my "Business Hall of Fame." He taught me the lessons of integrity, loyalty, good manners, and humility. Thanks to you, one and all.

In terms of my personal life, there are two huge influencers who have marked these pages. My dad taught me the lesson of generosity and responsibility. His word was truly his bond. Finally, there is

Marta Erhard, my wife and partner of more than thirty-five years. She has encouraged me from the get-go, sometimes led me where I thought I could not go, and been there for me, as the saying goes, "In sickness and in health."

I now return to what makes writing an acknowledgment so difficult. I am sure I have forgotten some Adored Leaders who have shaped my life and success. I apologize in advance and promise that I treasure what you have taught me.

NOTES

INTRODUCTION

1. Samuel I. Hayakawa, *Modern Guide to Synonyms and Related Words* (New York: Funk & Wagnalls, 1968) (emphasis added).
2. S. Ambrose, *Band of Brothers: E Company, 506th Regiment, 101st Airborne from Normandy to Hitler's Eagle's Nest* (New York: Touchstone, 2001).
3. L. Alexander, *Biggest Brother: The Life of Major Dick Winters, the Man Who Led the Band of Brothers* (New York: N.A.L. Caliber Publishing, 2005).
4. J. R. Wooden and S. Jamison, *Wooden: A Lifetime of Observations and Reflections On and Off the Court* (New York: Contemporary Books, 1997).

CHAPTER 2

1. Abrar Al-Heeti, "Americans Are Checking Their Phones Now More Than Ever, Report Says," CNET, November 12, 2018, https://www.cnet.com/news/americans -are-checking-their-phones-now-more-than-ever-report-says/.
2. R. Oldenburg, *The Great Good Place: Cafes, Coffee Shops, Community Centers, Beauty Parlors, General Stores, Bars, Hangouts and How They Get You Through the Day* (New York: Marlowe & Company, 1989).
3. E. Becker, *The Denial of Death* (New York: The Free Press, 1973).
4. Marguerite Ward, "Why PepsiCo CEO Indra Nooyi Writes Letters to Her Employees' Parents," CNBC Make It, February 1, 2017, https://www.cnbc.com /2017/02/01/why-pepsico-ceo-indra-nooyi-writes-letters-to-her-employees -parents.html.
5. Marillyn Hewson, "The 4 Traits You Need to Be a Great Leader," *Fortune*, October 18, 2016, https://fortune.com/2016/10/18/mpw-leadership-lockheed-martin/.

CHAPTER 3

1. J. R. Wooden and S. Jamison, *Wooden: A Lifetime of Observations and Reflections On and Off the Court* (New York: Contemporary Books, 1997) (emphasis added).
2. Wooden and Jamison, *Wooden*.
3. J. Mattis and B. West, *Call Sign Chaos: Learning to Lead* (New York: Random House, 2019), p. 13.

CHAPTER 4

1. Steve Allen, quoted in P. L. Berman, *Courage of Conviction* (New York: Dodd, Mead & Company, 1985), p. 8.
2. J. R. Wooden and S. Jamison, *Wooden: A Lifetime of Observations and Reflections On and Off the Court* (New York: Contemporary Books, 1997).
3. H. Gardner, *Leading Minds: An Anatomy of Leadership* (New York: Basic Books, 1995).
4. S. L. Carter, *Integrity* (New York: HarperCollins, 1996).
5. Kevin J. Ryan, "23andMe's Anne Wojcicki Says Doing These 2 Things as a Leader Built Her Company's Culture of Honesty," *Inc.*, March/April 2019, https://www.inc.com/mbvans/contest.html.
6. J. B. Peterson, *12 Rules for Life: An Antidote to Chaos* (Toronto: Random House Canada, 2018), p. 203.
7. L. Kohlberg, C. Levine, and A. Hewer, "Moral Stages: A Current Formulation and a Response to Critics," *Contributions to Human Development* 10 (1983): 174; J. Piaget, "Piaget's Theory," in *Childhood Cognitive Development: The Essential Readings*, ed. K. Lee (Malden, MA: Blackwell Publishers, 2000).

CHAPTER 5

1. J. Greenberg (ed.), *Insidious Workplace Behavior* (Milton Park, UK: Taylor and Francis, 2010).
2. A. Comte-Sponville, *A Small Treatise on the Great Virtues: The Use of Philosophy in Everyday Life* (New York: Picador, 2002). While not an easy book to read due to the depth of the scholarship, it is a wonderfully useful introduction to the ideals of human goodness. Besides that, it's beautifully written.
3. R. A. Heinlein, *Friday* (Rockville, MD: Phoenix Pick, 2017), p. 253
4. L. M. Anderson and C. M. Pearson, "Tit for Tat? The Spiraling Effect of Incivility in the Workplace," *Academy of Management Review* 24, no. 3 (1999): 452–471.

CHAPTER 7

1. Carl Sahlsten, in communication to author.

CHAPTER 9

1. T. DeCotiis, *Make It Glow: How to Build a Company Reputation for Human Goodness, Flawless Execution, and Being Best-In-Class* (Austin: Greenleaf Book Group, 2008).
2. Homebuilding Partners, "Our Foundations" (vision statement), 2014.

3. Catherine Clifford, "Elon Musk: This is the 'Why' of Tesla," CNBC Make It, CNBC.com, February 4, 2019, https://www.cnbc.com/2019/02/04/elon-musk-on-the-why-and-purpose-behind-tesla.html.

4. M. Whitman and J. O'C Hamilton, *The Power of Many: Values for Success in Business and Life* (New York: Crown, 2010).

5. Mission BBQ, "Giving Back," https://mission-bbq.com/.

6. Mission BBQ, "Giving Back," https://mission-bbq.com/giving-back.

7. C. T. Sullivan, "A Stake in the Business," *Harvard Business Review* 83, no. 9 (September 2005): 1–8.

8. BKS-Partners, Inc., "Our Firm," https://bks-partners.com/our-firm/why-bks/.

9. Ruth's Chris Hospitality Group, Inc., vision statement.

CHAPTER 10

1. D. K. Goodwin, *Team of Rivals: The Political Genius of Abraham Lincoln* (New York: Simon and Shuster, 2005). Without question, this book is one of the best books on leadership that I have ever read.

2. Georgia Wells, "Facebook Doesn't Want to Censor Political Ads Over Accuracy, Executive Says," *The Wall Street Journal*, October 22, 2019, https://www.wsj.com/articles/facebook-doesnt-want-to-censor-political-ads-over-accuracy-executive-says-11571720440.

3. "Twitter to Ban All Political Advertising," BBC News, October 31, 2019, https://www.bbc.com/news/world-us-canada-50243306.

4. Dana Hughes, "Bill Clinton Regrets Rwanda Now (Not So Much In 1994)," ABC News, February 28, 2014, https://abcnews.go.com/blogs/politics/2014/02/bill-clinton-regrets-rwanda-now-not-so-much-in-1994.

5. T. DeCotiis, *Why Good People Can't Even Agree to Disagree: Some Thoughts on Human Goodness* (Colorado Springs: Corvirtus, 2015).

6. A. Comte-Sponville, *A Small Treatise on the Great Virtues: The Use of Philosophy in Everyday Life* (New York: Picador, 2002), 266.

7. C. Peterson and M. E. P. Seligman, *Character Strengths and Virtues: A Handbook and Classification* (New York: Oxford University Press, 2004). The "Big Six" definitions are derived from Peterson and Seligman's book, but with some changes to reflect my experience.

8. BJ Fogg, *Tiny Habits: The Small Changes That Change Everything* (Boston: Houghton Mifflin Harcourt, 2020).

9. A. Maslow, "Neurosis as a Failure of Personal Growth," *Humanitas* 3 (1967): 153–169 (emphasis added).

AUTHOR'S REQUEST

Please go to Amazon and rate this book and give it a review. If you recommend the book, your friends will be grateful for your solid recommendation. If you don't like the book, they will feel the same way—grateful that they did not waste their time. Honesty is always a win-win situation.

ABOUT THE AUTHOR

Tom DeCotiis' first leadership gig was as the owner of a hamburger stand on the border between the Inglewood and Watts neighborhoods of Los Angeles, California. When the Watts riot of August 1965 occurred, his business almost didn't survive. Everyone was afraid, many were armed, and life seemed to hit pause. With his team's help, Tom was able to rebuild the business to where it had been before the riots. It was a difficult time, but he learned a lot and good things came from the experience. For example, Tom acquired a much deeper appreciation for what people need at the level of their DNA: *to belong and to have significance.* This experience led him to complete his education. Tom went on to earn an MBA from California State University, Long Beach, and a PhD from the University of Wisconsin, Madison, and, from there, to appointments on the graduate faculties of Cornell University and the Daria Moore School of Business at the University of South Carolina.

Since that time, Tom has had many leadership roles. He was a member of IBM's advisory board during its turnaround days and served on the board of several not-for-profit organizations and a couple of for-profit companies. He was a trusted advisor to the leaders of several companies and non-profit organizations and had direct involvement in the founding of several companies. He was also a member of the turnaround teams at Greyhound Bus Lines and Darden Restaurants, and co-founded Corvirtus, a company that has thrived for more than forty years.

Tom has published more than 100 articles and one other book: *Make It Glow: How to Build a Company Reputation for Human Goodness, Flawless Execution, and Being Best-in-Class.*